TEACHER'S PET PUBLICATIONS

LITPLAN TEACHER PACK
for
Beowulf
as translated by
Burton Raffel

Written by
Joan Wallace

© 2005 Teacher's Pet Publications
All Rights Reserved

This LitPlan for
Beowulf
has been brought to you by Teacher's Pet Publications, Inc.

Copyright Teacher's Pet Publications 2006

Only the student materials in this unit plan (such as worksheets, study questions, and tests) may be reproduced multiple times for use in the purchaser's classroom.

For any additional copyright questions,
contact Teacher's Pet Publications.

www.tpet.com

TABLE OF CONTENTS - *Beowulf*

Introduction	5
Unit Objectives	7
Reading Assignment Sheet	8
Unit Outline	9
Study Questions (Short Answer)	13
Quiz/Study Questions (Multiple Choice)	27
Pre-reading Vocabulary Worksheets	55
Lesson One (Introductory Lesson)	69
Nonfiction Assignment Sheet	78
Oral Reading Evaluation Form	82
Writing Assignment 1	75
Writing Assignment 2	84
Writing Assignment 3	94
Writing Evaluation Form	76
Vocabulary Review Activities	92
Extra Writing Assignments/Discussion ?s	87
Unit Review Activities	97
Unit Tests	101
Unit Resource Materials	133
Vocabulary Resource Materials	155

A FEW NOTES ABOUT *BEOWULF*'S ORIGINS

Beowulf is widely believed to be the oldest surviving poem in any modern European language. It is most likely the sole survivor of what many scholars believe was a thriving epic tradition dating from the sixth and seventh centuries. Originally composed in the oral tradition, the *Beowulf* epic provides us with valuable insights into the traditions and values of the early Norse peoples of the North Atlantic region. It is assumed that the epic began as a pagan account of national history and heroism. Some time in the ninth century *Beowulf* was written down in the Old English dialect, recorded by Christian monks in England from that era. The poem exists today as a hybrid piece—retaining pagan and feudal remnants while assuming a language that is newly Christian. Epic poetry was the genre of choice for early Europeans, lending itself to oral repetition and storytelling.

A sole copy of *Beowulf* not only survived Henry VIII's destruction of the Catholic monasteries in the sixteen century, but also escaped serious harm during a 1731 fire that ravaged the British Museum, where it can be viewed today in the library of the British Museum in London.

The Burton Raffel translation is widely regarded as the definitive edition of the first English epic.

-From the Introduction to *Beowulf* by Burton Raffel

INTRODUCTION

This LitPlan has been designed to develop students' reading, writing, thinking, and language skills through exercises and activities related to *Beowulf*. It includes 18 lessons, supported by extra resource materials.

The **introductory lesson** introduces students to the historical background of the time in which the epic, *Beowulf*, was composed. Following the introductory activity, students are given a transition to explain how the activity relates to the book they are about to read. Following the transition, students are given the materials they will be using during the unit. At the end of the lesson, students begin the pre-reading work for the first reading assignment.

The **reading assignments** are approximately thirty pages each; some are a little shorter while others are a little longer. Students have approximately 15 minutes of pre-reading work to do prior to each reading assignment. This pre-reading work involves reviewing the study questions for the assignment and doing some vocabulary work for 8 to 10 vocabulary words they will encounter in their reading.

The **study guide questions** are fact-based questions; students can find the answers to these questions right in the text. These questions come in two formats: short answer or multiple choice. The best use of these materials is probably to use the short answer version of the questions as study guides for students (since answers will be more complete), and to use the multiple choice version for occasional quizzes.

The **vocabulary work** is intended to enrich students' vocabularies as well as to aid in the students' understanding of the book. Prior to each reading assignment, students will complete a two-part worksheet for approximately 8 to 10 vocabulary words in the upcoming reading assignment. Part I focuses on students' use of general knowledge and contextual clues by giving the sentence in which the word appears in the text. Students are then to write down what they think the words mean based on the words' usage. Part II nails down the definitions of the words by giving students dictionary definitions of the words and having students match the words to the correct definitions based on the words' contextual usage. Students should then have an understanding of the words when they meet them in the text.

After each reading assignment, students will go back and formulate answers for the study guide questions. Discussion of these questions serves as a **review** of the most important events and ideas presented in the reading assignments.

After students complete reading the work, there is a **vocabulary review** lesson which pulls together all of the fragmented vocabulary lists for the reading assignments and gives students a review of all of the words they have studied.

Following the vocabulary review, a lesson is devoted to the **extra discussion questions/writing assignments**. These questions focus on interpretation, critical analysis and personal response, employing a variety of thinking skills and adding to the students' understanding of the novel.

There is a **group theme project** in which students will work in small groups to discuss several of the important themes relating to Anglo-Saxon society and their manifestation in *Beowulf*. Using information they have acquired through reading assignments and class discussions, students will meet in groups to discuss the Anglo-Saxon societal influences in *Beowulf*.

There are three **writing assignments** in this unit, each with the purpose of informing, persuading, or having students express personal opinions. The first assignment is to inform: students compose an essay in which they illustrate how Beowulf exemplifies the features of a literary epic. The second assignment is to persuade: students pretend to be Grendel's mother, writing a persuasive journal entry that describes the action and events from her perspective. The third assignment gives students the opportunity to express their personal ideas: they are to write a composition in which they identify what passions or qualities that they possess that if fostered could lead to them living in fame after their deaths.

There is a **nonfiction reading assignment**. Students are required to read articles or chapters relating to the time in which the epic, *Beowulf,* was written, and to gather information about the nature of the Anglo-Saxon people and how the history in this text relates to the accounts in *Beowulf*.

The **review lesson** pulls together all of the aspects of the unit. The teacher is given four or five choices of activities or games to use which all serve the same basic function of reviewing all of the information presented in the unit.

The **unit test** comes in two formats: multiple choice or short answer. As a convenience, two different tests for each format have been included. There is also an advanced short answer unit test for advanced students.

There are additional **support materials** included with this unit. The **Unit Resource Materials** section includes suggestions for an in-class library, crossword and word search puzzles related to the novel, and extra worksheets. There is a list of **bulletin board ideas** which gives the teacher suggestions for bulletin boards to go along with this unit. In addition, there is a list of **extra class activities** the teacher could choose from to enhance the unit or as a substitution for an exercise the teacher might feel is inappropriate for his/her class. **Answer keys** are located directly after the **reproducible student materials** throughout the unit. The **Vocabulary Resource Materials** section includes similar worksheets and games to reinforce the vocabulary words.

The **level** of this unit can be varied depending upon the criteria on which the individual assignments are graded, the teacher's expectations of his/her students in class discussions, and the formats chosen for the study guides, quizzes and test. If teachers have other ideas/activities they wish to use, they can usually easily be inserted prior to the review lesson.

UNIT OBJECTIVES – *Beowulf*

1. Through reading *Beowulf*, students will gain a better understanding of the importance of heroism, courage and camaraderie to the early Anglo-Saxon peoples, and how their views on these traits continue to inform western thinking.

2. Students will demonstrate their understanding of the text on four levels: factual, interpretive, critical and personal.

3. Students will discuss the features of a literary epic and how these features are evident in *Beowulf*.

4. Students will be given the opportunity to practice reading aloud and silently to improve their skills in each area.

5. Students will answer questions to demonstrate their knowledge and understanding of the main events and characters in *Beowulf* as they relate to the author's theme development.

6. Students will enrich their vocabularies and improve their understanding of the novel through the vocabulary lessons prepared for use in conjunction with the novel.

7. The writing assignments in this unit are geared to several purposes:
    a. To have students demonstrate their abilities to inform, to persuade, or to express their own personal ideas
        Note: Students will demonstrate ability to write effectively to <u>inform</u> by developing and organizing facts to convey information. Students will demonstrate the ability to write effectively to <u>persuade</u> by selecting and organizing relevant information, establishing an argumentative purpose, and by designing an appropriate strategy for an identified audience. Students will demonstrate the ability to write effectively to <u>express personal ideas</u> by selecting a form and its appropriate elements.
    b. To check the students' reading comprehension
    c. To make students think about the ideas presented by the novel
    d. To encourage logical thinking
    e. To provide an opportunity to practice good grammar and improve students' use of the English language.

8. Students will read aloud, report, and participate in large and small group discussions to improve their public speaking and personal interaction skills.

READING ASSIGNMENT SHEET - *Beowulf*

Date Assigned	Chapters Assigned	Completion Date
	Introduction	
	Prologue through Chapter 13	
	Chapters 14 through 25	
	Chapters 26 through 35	
	Chapters 36 through 43	

UNIT OUTLINE - *Beowulf*

1 Introduction	2 Introduction PVR "Raffel's Introduction to *Beowulf*"	3 Study Questions – "Raffel's Introduction to Beowulf" PVR Prologue through Chapter 13	4 Writing Assignment 1 Review literary terms Study Questions Prologue through Chapter 13	5 Quiz on Prologue through Chapter 13 Library Research PVR Chapters 14-25
6 Continue Library Research	7 Study Questions Chapters 14-25 PV Chapters 26-35	8 Quiz on Chapters 14-25 Present Library Research	9 R Chapters 26-35	10 Study Questions Chapters 26-35 PVR Chapters 36-43
11 Finish Oral Reading- Chapters 36-43 Assign Writing Assignment #2	12 Complete Writing Assignment #2	13 Study Questions Chapters 36-43 Extra Group Discussion	14 Extra Group Discussion and Library Research	15 Vocabulary Review
16 Writing Assignment #3	17 Review	18 Test		

Key: P = Preview Study Questions V = Vocabulary Work R = Read

STUDY GUIDE QUESTIONS

SHORT ANSWER STUDY GUIDE QUESTIONS - *Beowulf*
(The answer can be found in the chapter number in parenthesis)

Introduction
1. Why does the editor refer to the *Beowulf* epic as "essentially an aristocratic poem"? (I)
2. What were the basic virtues prized by Anglo-Saxon society? (I)
3. Account for the sharp descriptions of the scenes in *Beowulf*. (I)
4. How is *Beowulf* drawn from both the pagan and the Christian traditions? (I)

Prologue - Chapter 13
1. Why does Hrothgar decide to build a mighty hall? What does he call it? Describe this hall. (1)
2. Describe what transpires in the mead hall to evoke the anger of the monster. (1)
3. What is Grendel's lineage? Why is he described as being "born of Cain"? (1)
4. Why has Grendel been exiled? (1)
5. What happens during Grendel's first visit to Herot? When does this occur? Describe the scene. (2)
6. How long does Grendel haunt Herot? (2)
7. Why doesn't Grendel attack Hrothgar? (2)
8. To what measures do Hrothgar and his nobles resort to rid themselves of Grendel? (2)
9. How does Beowulf react when he hears of the plight of the Danes and Hrothgar? (3)
10. How are Beowulf and his men received when they arrive on the Danish shore? (3)
11. Why does Beowulf describe himself by recounting his heritage? Why has he come? (4)
12. How does the watchman respond to Beowulf's explanation of why they have come to the rescue of the Danes? (4)
13. Hrothgar's herald greets Beowulf and his men. According to the herald, what distinguishes Beowulf's visit from those of others who have come before him? (5)
14. Who is Wulfgar? What role does he play in this chapter? (5)
15. According to Wulfgar, why have Beowulf and his men come all the way from Geatland to help the Danes? (6)
16. Describe Beowulf's boasts upon meeting Hrothgar, King of the Danes. (6)
17. What one request does Beowulf make of Hrothgar? (6)
18. If Beowulf loses the battle with Grendel, what are his instructions for after his death? (6)
19. How did Hrothgar become king? What is his past relationship to the Geats? (7)
20. What is the purpose of the feast that Hrothgar hosts in Beowulf's honor? (7)
21. Identify Unferth. Why does he seem to be perplexed by Beowulf's stories? How does he address Beowulf? (8)
22. Describe Unferth's tale of the swimming competition between Brecca and Beowulf. (8)
23. What is Beowulf's response to Unferth? (8)
24. Beowulf continues with his story, countering Unferth's tale. How does his tale end? (9)
25. Describe Welthow. (9)
26. What is Hrothgar's declaration to Beowulf at the end of Chapter 9? (9)

Beowulf Study Questions Page 2

27. Beowulf and his men move into Herot for the night while Hrothgar sleeps peacefully. What is Beowulf's boast? (10)
28. What do Beowulf's men think of their chances against Grendel? (10)
29. How does Grendel respond when he comes to Herot? Describe his reaction to seeing the sleeping Geats. (11)
30. What happens when Grendel reaches for Beowulf? (11)
31. Describe the struggles that ensues between Beowulf and Grendel. (11)
32. What happens when Beowulf's men attack Grendel? Account for this outcome to their efforts. (12)
33. At the conclusion of the battle between Beowulf and Grendel, what transpires? (12)
34. On the morning following the battle, describe the reactions of Hrothgar's people. (13)
35. Describe the lake into which Grendel vanished. (13)
36. Who is Siegmund? Why is his story recounted? (13)

Chapters 14 -25
1. Upon seeing Grendel's bloody arm swinging high from the "gold-shining roof" of Herot, what is Hrothgar's proclamation? (14)
2. Describe Unferth's reaction to seeing the arm of Grendel. (14)
3. What were Hrothgar's gifts to Beowulf for removing the threat of Grendel to the Danes? (15)
4. What gifts does Hrothgar give to Beowulf's men? (16)
5. How were the bodies of the dead disposed of in Anglo-Saxon times? (16)
6. Who are the two sons of Hrothgar and Welthow? Why are they permitted at the victory feast? (17)
7. What gifts does Welthow give to Beowulf at the feast? What are her words to Beowulf about her sons? (18)
8. Why did the Danes sleep with their armor on? (18)
9. How long had Grendel's mother dwelt in the cold, murky subterranean lake? (19)
10. What is Grendel's mother's motive in coming to Herot? (19)
11. Whom does she snatch? (19)
12. What individuals had witnessed the two fiends prior to the time of the attacks on Herot? (20)
13. Describe the location of the place where Grendel lived with his mother. (20)
14. According to Beowulf, —what is the only thing that survives death? (21)
15. What do Hrothgar's men discover on their search for Grendel's mother? (21)
16. Describe the lake that serves as the entrance to Grendel's mother's lair. (21)
17. What equipment does Beowulf adorn as he goes in pursuit of Grendel's mother? How is this different from what he wore in his battle with Grendel? (21)
18. What is the significance of the sword, Hrunting? (21)
19. Describe the encounter Beowulf has with Grendel's mother. How effective were his weapons? (22)

Beowulf Study Questions Page 3

20. How does Beowulf eventually slay Grendel's mother? (23)
21. What does Beowulf do with the body of Grendel that he finds lying in a corner of the lair? (23)
22. What is happening on the surface with Hrothgar's men while Beowulf is fighting under the lake? (23)
23. What happens to the "magnificent sword"? (23)
24. What does Beowulf take with him as souvenirs of his victory over Grendel's mother? (23)
25. What "trophy" does Beowulf give to Hrothgar as a symbol of his victory over the demons? (23)
26. To what does Beowulf attribute his victory over Grendel's mother in his audience with Hrothgar? (24)
27. Describe Hrothgar's reaction to what is written on the hilt of the sword. What is it? (24)
28. What has Hrothgar to say of the role of pride for a leader? (25)
29. Before Beowulf and his men set sail on their return home, Unferth approaches Beowulf and offers him a gift. What is it? Explain its significance. (25)

Chapters 26-35
1. What is Beowulf's vow to the Danes prior to his departure? (26)
2. Describe Hrothgar's final words to Beowulf. What realization does the old king make? (26)
3. Describe Higlac's queen. How is she received by the Geats? (27)
4. Describe Beowulf's account of his adventures that he relates to his king, Higlac. (28)
5. Why might Ingeld and his followers be angry at seeing Beowulf's ancestral armor and weapons? (29)
6. Why is this chapter devoted to the re-telling of the tale of Beowulf's victories over Grendel and his mother? (30)
7. How does Higlac reward Beowulf for his feats? (31)
8. Who is king after Higlac? How does he die? (31)
9. What large event happens fifty years into Beowulf's reign? (31)
10. Why did the slave steal from the dragon? What was his motivations? (32)
11. How did the dragon's tower come to have so many riches? (32)
12. Describe how the dragon discovered the riches. (32)
13. What does Beowulf think has brought on the wrath of the dragon? (33)
14. Describe the dragon's "hidden home". (34)
15. Why does Beowulf again recount the glory of day's past before taking on a battle with the dragon? (34)
16. How does Beowulf feel about his upcoming battle against the dragon? (34)
17. Why does Beowulf announce that he is going to face the dragon alone? (35)
18. What do Beowulf's men do as he is taking on the dragon? (35)

Beowulf Study Questions Page 4

Chapters 36-43
1. Identify: Wiglaf. (36)
2. What prior battle experience has Wiglaf experienced? (36)
3. Describe the effectiveness of Beowulf's sword, Nagling. (36)
4. Describe how Beowulf and Wiglaf join forces to slay the dragon. (37)
5. What is Beowulf's dying wish? (37)
6. How does Beowulf react when he sees the treasure? (38)
7. What are his funeral instructions? Why? (38)
8. After both Beowulf and the dragon are slain, how do Beowulf's followers behave? What does Wiglaf say to them? (39)
9. According to the messenger who announces Beowulf's death to his people, what might the Geats expect now from their enemies? (40)
10. Wiglaf decrees that all the treasure should be burned. What is his reason for this? (41)
11. What role does fate play in Beowulf's demise, according to Wiglaf? (42)
12. What do the Geats do with the dragon's body? (42)
13. Describe Beowulf's funeral pyre. (43)
14. What is the role of the twelve horsemen who surround Beowulf's monument? (43)

ANSWER KEY SHORT ANSWER STUDY GUIDE QUESTIONS – *Beowulf*

Introduction
1. Why does the editor refer to the *Beowulf* epic as "essentially an aristocratic poem"?
    Beowulf is concerned mainly with the large issues of kings and kingship. The other classes of society are not represented.

2. What were the basic virtues prized by the Anglo-Saxons?
    Strength, courage, bravery, and generosity were the virtues prized by the Anglo-Saxons.

3. Account for the sharp descriptions of the scenes in *Beowulf*.
    Beowulf began in the oral tradition—meant to be heard rather than read, therefore the early poet-singers felt compelled to use particularly graphic descriptions of scenes in order for the listeners to visualize the words.

4. How is Beowulf drawn from both the pagan and the Christian traditions?
    Originally composed in pre-Christian England, the poem began as a pagan piece with interjections of monsters and ominous forces. The poem actually was first written by Christian monks who superimposed Christian sentiments over the largely pagan, supernatural story.

Prologue-Chapter 13
1. Why does Hrothgar decide to build a mighty hall? What does he call it? Describe this hall.
    After Hrothgar led the Danes to victory, he commemorated his victory by building a mighty mead hall. He called the hall Herot. Herot is described as "the most beautiful if dwellings," one that would reach high toward the heavens.

2. Describe what transpired in the mead hall to evoke the anger of the monster.
    The monster dwelling down in the darkness is angered by the music in the hall, by the song of the poet retelling the history of the Danes, and by the sounds of rejoicing.

3. What is Grendel's lineage? Why is he described as being "born of Cain"?
    Grendel is described as being spawned in slime by two of the monsters who were descendants of the Biblical character, Cain, who was banished from God for committing the murder of his brother, Abel.

4. Why has Grendel been exiled?
    Grendel has been exiled, together with all monsters, goblins, and forms of evil-by the Almighty—condemned to live beneath the earth.

5. What happens during Grendel's first visit to Herot?
    Grendel finds Hrothgar's men asleep in the Herot. He snatched up thirty men, smashed them and ran out with their bodies.

6. How long does Grendel haunt Herot?
    For twelve winters Grendel terrorizes Hrothgar's mead hall.

7. Why doesn't Grendel attack Hrothgar?
    Grendel does not dare to touch Hrothgar as the king is protected by God.

8. To what measures do Hrothgar and his nobles resort to rid themselves of Grendel?
    Hrothgar and his men resort to sacrificing to "the old stone gods" and "hoping for Hell's support" to rid themselves of Grendel.

9. How does Beowulf react when he hears of the plight of the Danes and Hrothgar?
    Beowulf reacts to the news that Hrothgar and the Danes have been attacked by Grendel by selecting the bravest of soldiers in Geatland and traveling across the seas to help.

10. How are Beowulf and his men received when they arrive on the Danish shore?
    The arrival of Beowulf and his men surprises Hrothgar's lieutenant who is guarding the shore. Because there is not prior announcement of their arrival, the lieutenant demands to know their business before they can proceed.

11. Why does Beowulf describe himself by recounting his heritage? Why has he come?
    Beowulf draws a connection between himself and his present purpose and the Danish people by reviewing his ancestry which appeared in the oral tradition as common knowledge. Beowulf has come to help drive out Grendel.

12. How does the watchman respond to Beowulf's explanation of why they have come to rescue the Danes?
    The watchman believes Beowulf and decides to escort him, himself, to the court of Hrothgar.

13. Hrothgar's herald greets Beowulf and his men. According to the herald, what distinguishes Beowulf's visit from those others who have come before him?
    Beowulf's visit is distinguished from others by the fact that Beowulf acts freely and boldly, and very courageously.

14. Who is Wulfgar? What role does he play in this chapter?
    Wulfgar was a noble Swede, known for his strength and wisdom. Wulfgar offers to introduce Beowulf and his men to Hrothgar, King of the Danes.

15. According to Wulfgar, why have Beowulf and his men come all the way from Geatland to help the Danes?
    According to Wulfgar, God has sent Beowulf on his mission to help the Danes defeat Grendel.

16. Describe Beowulf's boasts upon meeting Hrothgar, King of the Danes.
    Beowulf greets Hrothgar by regaling him with stories of his great strength and prior exploits. Beowulf drove five giants into chains and chased them from the earth, and has hunted monsters out of the ocean.

17. What one request does Beowulf make of Hrothgar?
    Beowulf asks Hrothgar to allow him and his men alone to drive Grendel from Herot.

18. If Beowulf loses the battle with Grendel, what are his instructions for after his death?
    Beowulf tells Hrothgar that if Grendel defeats him, the Danish king should send the mail of his armor to Higlac, and return the inheritance he had received from Hrethel.

19. How did Hrothgar become king? What is his past relationship to the Geats?
    Hrothgar's older brother, Hergar, was king and died, making Hrothgar king. Hrothgar worked with Beowulf's father, Edgetho, to secure an earlier peace.

20. What is the purpose of the feast that Hrothgar hosts in Beowulf's honor?
    Hrothgar hosts a feast to honor Beowulf and his men before they head off to face Grendel.

21. Identify Unferth. Why does he seem to be perplexed by Beowulf's stories? How does he address Beowulf?
    Unferth is a Danish nobleman who is angry that any warrior anywhere has achieved greater glory than he has. Unferth calls Beowulf a "boastful fool".

22. Describe Unferth's tale of the swimming competition between Brecca and Beowulf.
    Unferth tells the story of a swimming competition between Beowulf and Brecca that lasted for seven long nights and ended with the sea carrying Brecca home to victory—not far from the shores of his native Norway.

23. What is Beowulf's response to Unferth?
    Beowulf recounts that he swam side by side with Brecca for five nights until a storm carried him away where he was attacked by sea monsters. He killed nine monsters before washing up on a Finnish beach.

24. Beowulf continues with his story, countering Unferth's tale. How does his tale end?
    Beowulf explains that he killed many monsters and challenged Unferth to find any man—Brecca included—who could match his bravery.

25. Describe Welthow.
    Welthow is Hrothgar's "gold-ringed Queen." She is described as a noble woman who knows "what is right."

26. What is Hrothgar's declaration to Beowulf at the end of Chapter 9?
    Hrothgar tells Beowulf that no one has ever been granted the access to Herot that he is granting to the Geat warrior. He tells Beowulf to make Herot his own.

27. Beowulf and his men move into Herot for the night while Hrothgar sleeps peacefully. What is Beowulf's boast?
    Beowulf boasts that he will defeat Grendel with his bare hands.

28. What do Beowulf's men think of their chances against Grendel?
    The men believe they will never see their homeland again, that they will be defeated by Grendel.

29. How does Grendel respond when he comes to Herot? Describe his reaction to seeing the sleeping Geats.
    Grendel tears the hinges off the door at Herot and is thrilled at the sight of the sleeping Geats—expecting to fill his belly with their meat.

30. What happens when Grendel reaches for Beowulf?
    Beowulf grabs Grendel and begins a hand to hand battle with him.

31. Describe the struggle that ensues between Beowulf and Grendel.
    Herot trembles as Beowulf and Grendel fight to the death. Beowulf's prowess causes Grendel to shriek in agonizing pain.

32. What happens when Beowulf's men attack Grendel?
    Grendel bewitched the weapons of Beowulf's men; they are unable to hurt the monster.

33. At the conclusion of the battle between Beowulf and Grendel, what transpires?
    Grendel is no match for Beowulf, who rips the monster's arm from its socket and leaves Grendel mortally wounded, running back to his cave.

34. On the morning following the battle, describe the reactions of Hrothgar's people.
    They rejoiced with no sense of remorse for the monster's suffering.

35. Describe the lake into which Grendel vanished.
    The lake into which Grendel vanished was steaming and boiling with blood, and it was very wavy.

36. Who is Siegmund? Why is his story recounted?
    Siegmund was a legendary hero to the Danes. Tales of his exploits were passed down through generations. Beowulf's victory over Grendel was likened to Siegmund's great feats.

Chapters 14-25
1. Upon seeing Grendel's bloody arm swinging high from the "gold-shining roof" of Herot, what is Hrothgar's proclamation?
    Hrothgar is so overjoyed at the sight of Grendel's amputated arm and its implications, he makes Beowulf his own son and vows to forever preserve the peace between their people.

2. Describe Unferth's reaction to seeing the arm of Grendel.
    Upon seeing Grendel's arm, Unferth stops bragging, and he grows quiet, silenced by Beowulf's bravery.

3. What were Hrothgar's gifts to Beowulf for removing the threat of Grendel?
    For defeating Grendel, Beowulf is given a golden banner to commemorate his victory, a coat of mail, and an ancient sword.

4. What gifts does Hrothgar give to Beowulf's men?
    Hrothgar gives Beowulf's men ancient armor and swords.

5. How were the bodies of the dead disposed of in Anglo-Saxon times?
    In Anglo-Saxon times, the bodies of dead soldiers were burned on a funeral pyre.

6. Who are the two sons of Hrothgar and Welthow? Why are they permitted at the victory feast?
    Hrethric and Hrothmund are the sons of Hrothgar and Welthow. They are permitted at the feast because they are the guests of Beowulf.

7. What gifts does Welthow give to Beowulf at the feast? What are her words to Beowulf about her sons?
    Welthow give Beowulf a mail shirt, golden armbands, and "the most beautiful necklace known to men." She asks Beowulf to lend her two sons his wise and gentle heart.

8. Why did the Danes sleep with their armor on?
    It was the custom of the Danes to be ready for war.

9. How long had Grendel's mother dwelt in the cold, subterranean lake?
    Grendel's mother had lived in the lake since Cain killed his brother Abel.

10. What is Grendel's mother's motive in coming to Herot?
    Grendel's mother comes to Herot seeking revenge for the loss of her son.

11. Whom does she snatch?
    Grendel's mother snatches Hrothgar's closest friend, Esher.

12. What individuals had witnessed the two fiends prior to the time of the attacks on Herot?
    The peasants in the field had witnessed Grendel and his mother lurking in the darkness prior to the attacks.

13. Describe the location of the place where Grendel lived with his mother.
    Grendel and his mother lived beneath a lake covered with frozen spray. The lake burned "like a torch", and it was a lake rumored to be bottomless.

14. According to Beowulf, —what is the only thing that survives death?
    The only thing that survives death, according to Beowulf, is glory and fame.

15. What do Hrothgar's men discover on their search for Grendel's mother?
    Hrothgar's men find the bloody head of Esher on their way to search for Grendel's mother.

16. Describe the lake that serves as the entrance to Grendel's mother's cave.
    The boiling lake was crawling with sea serpents.

17. What equipment does Beowulf adorn as he goes in pursuit of Grendel's mother? How is this different from what he wore in his battle with Grendel?
    Beowulf adorned armor, chain mail, Hrothgar's helmet, and Unferth's sword. Beowulf wore no armor in his battle with Grendel.

18. What is the significance of the sword, Hrunting?
    Hrunting is the sword given to Beowulf by Unferth. It has a shining blade and was hardened in blood.

19. Describe the encounter Beowulf has with Grendel's mother. How effective were his weapons?
    After Beowulf swims for hours through the lake to her cave, his weapons were useless against Grendel's mother so he engages in hand-to-hand combat with her. She almost succeeded in stabbing Beowulf but his chain mail saved him.

20. How does Beowulf eventually slay Grendel's mother?
    Beowulf discovers a sword hanging on the wall of the cave and slices her neck through.

21. What does Beowulf do with the body of Grendel that he finds lying in the corner of the lair?
    After finding Grendel's body, Beowulf cuts his head off.

22. What is happening on the surface with Hrothgar's men while Beowulf is fighting under the lake?
    Hrothgar's men on the surface speak of Beowulf as a warrior who has died in battle. They have lost hope in his return.

23. What happens to the "magnificent sword"?
    The "magnificent sword" melted.

24. What does Beowulf take with him as souvenirs of his victory over Grendel's mother?
    As souvenirs of his victory, Beowulf takes Grendel's head and the hilt of the "magnificent sword".

25. What "trophy" does Beowulf give to Hrothgar as a symbol of his victory over the demons?
    Beowulf presents Hrothgar with Grendel's head as a symbol of his victory.

26. To what does Beowulf attribute his victory over Grendel's mother in his audience with Hrothgar?
    Beowulf attributes his victory to God's grace.

27. Describe Hrothgar's reaction to what is written on the hilt of the sword. What is it?
    Hrothgar stares in amazement at the hilt of this sword that was forged by giants and monsters. Its original owner's name is inscribed, as are stories of ancient wars between good and evil.

28. What has Hrothgar to say of the role of pride for a leader?
    Hrothgar cautions Beowulf against excessive pride and to realize that all glory is owed to God.

29. Before Beowulf and his men set sail on their return home, Unferth approaches Beowulf and offers him a gift. What is it? Explain its significance.
    Unferth gives Beowulf the gift of his sword, Hrunting. This is the sword Unferth had boasted of earlier in his verbal bantering with Beowulf.

Chapter 26 -35
1. What is Beowulf's vow to the Danes prior to his departure?
   Beowulf tells the Danes that if he ever hears again that they are threatened; he will come to their aid.

2. Describe Hrothgar's final words to Beowulf. What realization does the old king make?
   Hrothgar tells Beowulf that the peace that he has brought to the Danes will last as long as Hrothgar lives and that the Geats and Danes shall always be friends. Hrothgar realizes, however, that he is likely never to see Beowulf again.

3. Describe Higlac's queen. How is she received by the Geats?
   Higd was Higlac's young wife who was wise and knowing beyond her years. She is highly received by the Geats.

4. Describe Beowulf's account of his adventures that he relates to his king, Higlac.
   Beowulf tells his king, Higlac, that he saved the Danes from certain slaughter and that he was received as a son by Hrothgar.

5. Why might Ingeld and his followers be angry at seeing Beowulf's ancestral armor and weapons?
   Ingeld suggests that Beowulf's ancestral armor was involved in the slaying of Danes generations before.

6. Why is this chapter devoted to the re-telling of the tale of Beowulf's victories over Grendel and his mother?
   The re-telling of the victories that Beowulf experienced over Grendel and his mother serve to immortalize Beowulf's fame through the repetition of these tales of glory.

7. How does Higlac reward Beowulf for his feats?
   Higlac rewards Beowulf by giving him Beowulf's grandfather's ancestral sword, in addition to seven thousand hides of land.

8. Who is king after Higlac? How does he die?
   Higlac's son, Herdred, succeeds him to the throne. He is killed in a battle with the Swedes.

9. What large event happens fifty years into Beowulf's reign?
   After fifty years on the throne, Beowulf is faced with an awakening dragon that has come to terrorize the Geats.

10. Why did the slave steal from the dragon? What was his motivation?
    The slave stole from the dragon, not from desire but from need.

11. How did the dragon's tower come to have so many riches?
    The treasure guarded by the dragon came from the last survivor of a noble race.

12. Describe how the dragon discovered the riches.
    After the great warrior died, a dragon seeking shelter found the treasure and stayed to guard it.

13. What does Beowulf think has brought on the wrath of the dragon?
    Beowulf felt that because he as a king had broken God's law, the dragon wreaked his wrath upon the Geats.

14. Describe the dragon's "hidden home."
    The dragon's "hidden home" was enclosed by giant stones set deep in the ground with water beating on rocks close by.

15. Why does Beowulf again recount the glory of his day's past before taking on a battle with the dragon?
    Beowulf reviews his accomplishments prior to the battle with the dragon, as if to underscore his worthiness to take on this foe.

16. How does Beowulf feel about his upcoming battle against the dragon?
    Beowulf's heart was heavy, and he had a sense of doom prior to meeting the dragon in battle.

17. Why does Beowulf announce that he is going to fight the dragon alone?
    Beowulf tells the Geats that in every battle his place was in the front, alone, and so shall it be against the dragon.

18. What do Beowulf's men do as he is taking on the dragon?
    Beowulf's followers ran for their lives as their leader took on the dragon.

Chapter 36-43
1. Identify: Wiglaf.
    Wiglaf was a brave soldier who came to the assistance of Beowulf.

2. What prior battle experience has Wiglaf experienced?
    Wiglaf was an unseasoned warrior but a good soldier.

3. Describe the effectiveness of Beowulf's sword, Nagling.
    Beowulf's sword is destroyed by the dragon.

4. Describe how Beowulf and Wiglaf join forces to slay the dragon.
    Wiglaf struck at the dragon's lower half while Beowulf engaged the fire of the dragon. While Wiglaf distracted the dragon, Beowulf split the beast in two.

5. What is Beowulf's dying wish?
    Before he dies, Beowulf wishes to see the dragon's treasure—what he has died for.

6. How does Beowulf react when he sees the treasure?
    Beowulf prays to God, thanking him for opportunity to bring this treasure to his people.

7. What are his funeral instructions? Why?
    Beowulf asks that the Geats build him a tall tomb so that all sailors who pass by on the sea will know that a great man is buried there.

8. After both Beowulf and the dragon are slain, how do Beowulf's followers behave? What does Wiglaf say to them?
    After the danger has past, Beowulf's cowardly followers come out of hiding. Wiglaf angrily tells them that they are a disgrace to their people.

9. According to the messenger who announces Beowulf's death to his people, what might the Geats expect now from their enemies?
    The messenger tells the Geats that they can expect bitter quarrels now with the Franks and the Frisians once word reaches them of Beowulf's death.

10. Wiglaf decrees that all the treasure should be burned. What is his reason for this?
    Wiglaf tells the people that no one living should enjoy the jewels; they are not worthy.

11. What role does fate play in Beowulf's demise, according to Wiglaf?
    Wiglaf tells the people that fate had the dragon in store for Beowulf. It was "meant to be."

12. What do the Geats do with the dragon's body?
    The Geats rolled the dragon's body off the cliff and into the sea.

13. Describe Beowulf's funeral pyre.
    Beowulf's is called the greatest of funeral pyres, heaven was said to have swallowed the smoke of his pyre.

14. What is the role of the twelve horsemen who surround Beowulf's monument?
    The twelve Geat horsemen who rode around Beowulf's monument told of his deeds and of the greatness of his glory so that all would remember the great Geat warrior.

STUDY GUIDE/QUIZ QUESTIONS - *Beowulf*
Multiple Choice Format

Introduction

1. Why does the editor refer to the *Beowulf* epic as "essentially an aristocratic poem"?
    A. Only the aristocracy passed the epic along in the oral tradition by having their "players" perform it.
    B. The poem is about the working middle class Anglo-Saxons.
    C. *Beowulf* is concerned mainly with the large issues of kings and kingship. The other classes of society are not represented.
    D. In our modern times, only the most well-educated people still read *Beowulf*; people of the middle and lower classes never read it.

2. What were the basic virtues prized by the Anglo-Saxons?
    A. Wealth and knowledge were the prized virtues.
    B. Strength, courage, bravery, and generosity were prized by the Anglo-Saxons.
    C. The Anglo-Saxons prized loyalty, industriousness, and bravery.
    D. Strength and kindness were virtues prized by the Anglo-Saxons.

3. Account for the sharp descriptions of the scenes in *Beowulf*.
    A. *Beowulf* began in the oral tradition—meant to be heard rather than read; therefore, the early poet-singers felt compelled to use particularly graphic descriptions of scenes so the listeners could visualize the words.
    B. The work was first written down in a Germanic language, and the graphic descriptions come from the first translations to a more modern English.
    C. The original work may or may not have had the sharp descriptions. We do know that Henry VIII liked the plays and stories performed for him to be melodramatic, and the only surviving manuscript of *Beowulf* is from this era. Whether graphic descriptions were "original" or done to suit Henry VIII is unknown.
    D. The graphic descriptions of the scenes were put in to help the "players," the theater-actors of the time, set the scenes for the stage.

4. How is *Beowulf* drawn from both the pagan and the Christian traditions?
    A. Henry VIII went on an anti-Christian campaign, destroying the monasteries and changing what little literature there was to suit his more pagan-minded philosophies. The monks who wrote down *Beowulf* were forced to play down the Christian elements by adding more pagan imagery.
    B. Pagans and Christians were mixed through the years; sometimes pagans would tell the story, and sometimes Christians would, so through the years of the oral tradition, the story picked up elements of both cultures.
    C. Christians were the first ones to tell the story of *Beowulf*, but the story changed as pagans began to tell the story, adding in elements of their beliefs.
    D. Originally composed in pre-Christian England, the poem began as a pagan piece with interjections of monsters and ominous forces. The poem actually was first written by Christian monks who superimposed Christian sentiments over the largely pagan, supernatural story.

Beowulf Multiple Choice Questions page 2
Prologue-Chapter 13

1. Why does Hrothgar decide to build a mighty hall? What does he call it?
    A. His first mead hall was too small for his increasing army. He called it Cain.
    B. He thought he needed a hall to match his important social status. He called it Hrothgar Hall.
    C. After Hrothgar led the Danes to victory, he commemorated his victory by building a mighty mead hall. He called the hall Herot.
    D. He wanted a manly place to entertain his military captains and the local nobles. He called it Herod.

2. Describe what transpired in the mead hall to evoke the anger of the monster.
    A. Hrothgar used Grendel's belongings in the construction of the hall.
    B. The monster dwelling down in the darkness is angered by the music in the hall, by the song of the poet retelling the history of the Danes, and by the sounds of rejoicing.
    C. The Danes bragged that they were stronger than Grendel.
    D. The poet was telling the stories of the defeats of Grendel, and the monster was angered by the Danes' laughing at his misfortune.

3. What is Grendel's lineage?
    A. Grendel is described as being spawned in slime by two of the monsters who were descendants of the Biblical character, Cain, who was banished from God for committing the murder of his brother, Abel.
    B. Grendel was a direct descendant of the beasts of the devil, Gnaumat and Herot.
    C. Grendel was a descendant of the monster of Loki.
    D. The Chimera mated with a monster named Herot, giving birth to Grendel (thus the reason for Hrothgar's naming the hall Herot Hall since Grendel lived below).

4. Why has Grendel been exiled?
    A. Grendel was exiled by God for killing Cain.
    B. Grendel has been exiled, together with all monsters, goblins, and forms of evil-by the Almighty—condemned to live beneath the earth.
    C. When Grendel's true lineage was discovered, he was exiled.
    D. Humans respected Grendel's greatness–even though he was a monster, he was a *Great Monster*. Rather than killing such a magnificent beast, those who had conquered him long ago sent him into exile, extracting from Grendel the promise that he would never inflict evil upon humans again.

Beowulf Multiple Choice Questions page 3
Prologue-Chapter 13

5. What happens during Grendel's first visit to Herot?
   A. Grendel finds Hrothgar's men asleep in the Herot. He snatches up thirty men, smashes them, and runs out with their bodies.
   B. He is awakened and angered by the merry-making in the hall, enters the hall, grabs the poet and several musician, and kills them.
   C. Grendel comes peacefully to the hall at first, but seeing Hrothgar, he begins seething and flies into a rage, killing many of the guests.
   D. When Gendel enters the hall, the men flee. Grendel eats all the food and destroys the hall.

6. How long does Grendel haunt Herot?
   A. Twelve months
   B. Two winters
   C. Twelve winters
   D. Two generations

7. Why doesn't Grendel attack Hrothgar?
   A. Hrothgar is protected by his army.
   B. Grendel knows Hrothgar is stronger.
   C. Hrothgar is protected by God.
   D. Grendel can't physically get to Hrothgar to attack him.

8. To what measures do Hrothgar and his nobles resort to rid themselves of Grendel?
   A. They invoke the king's sorcerer to put a spell on Grendel, which gives them the advantage in the fight.
   B. They bring in the high priest to rid Grendel of demons, and pray to God to help them.
   C. They call the name of Christ, and hold a crucifix up to push Grendel back. This gives them enough of a momentary advantage that they are able to kill him.
   D. They resort to sacrificing to "the old stone gods" and "hoping for Hell's support" to rid themselves of Grendel.

9. How does Beowulf react when he hears of the plight of the Danes and Hrothgar?
   A. Beowulf selects the bravest of soldiers in Geatland and travels across the seas to help.
   B. Beowulf sends a messenger to Hrothgar, telling of his willingness to help.
   C. Beowulf laughs, raises his mug, and offers a toast to the bravery of Hrothgar and the Danes.
   D. Beowulf vows revenge if Hrothgar kills Grendel.

Beowulf Multiple Choice Questions page 4
Prologue-Chapter 13

10. How are Beowulf and his men received when they arrive on the Danish shore?
    A. Hrothgar's officers treat them with disdain and indifference.
    B. They are welcomed and given a feast and a place to rest.
    C. Hrothgar's lieutenant demands to know their business before they can proceed.
    D. Hrothgar's men warn them about Grendel, advise them to return from whence they came, and order them to retreat immediately.

11. Why does Beowulf describe himself by recounting his heritage?
    A. Beowulf stalls for more time by recounting his heritage. He hopes that news will soon come that Hrothgar has already killed Grendel.
    B. Beowulf wants to impress those who do not know him, assert his authority so others will follow him into battle against Grendel, and make clear to all present that he alone deserves the honor of killing the monster.
    C. Beowulf draws a connection between himself and his present purpose and the Danish people by reviewing his ancestry which appeared in the oral tradition as common knowledge.
    D. Recounting one's heritage was the appropriate greeting among the Danes at that time.

12. How does the watchman respond to Beowulf's explanation of why they have come to rescue the Danes?
    A. The watchman believes Beowulf and decides to escort him, himself, to the court of Hrothgar.
    B. The watchman isn't sure what to believe, but decides he had better take Beowulf to talk with someone with more authority.
    C. The watchman explains to Beowulf that he cannot leave his post, and then he sends two other men to take Beowulf to Hrothgar.
    D. The watchman further detains Beowulf until his account can be verified.

13. Hrothgar's herald greets Beowulf and his men. According to the herald, what distinguishes Beowulf's visit from those others who have come before him?
    A. Beowulf has brought no gifts for Hrothgar; he left in such a hurry that he forgot to bring the customary gifts. Hrothgar didn't mind, but it did set this visit apart.
    B. None of the others ever brought all their best soldiers to assist Hrothgar.
    C. Beowulf did not send a messenger to announce his visit or get permission to come.
    D. Beowulf acts freely, boldly, and very courageously.

14. Who is Wulfgar? What role does he play in this chapter?
    A. Wulfgar is a noble Swede, known for his strength and wisdom. Wulfgar offers to introduce Beowulf and his men to Hrothgar, King of the Danes.
    B. Wulfgar is the captain of Hrothgar's army. He offers to help plan Grendel's defeat.
    C. Wulfgar is an honored guest of Hrothgar who offers Beowulf some good advice.
    D. Wulfgar is the high priest who blesses the armies and their mission to kill Grendel.

Beowulf Multiple Choice Questions page 5
Prologue-Chapter 13

15. According to Wulfgar, why have Beowulf and his men come all the way from Geatland to help the Danes?
    A. Wulfgar believes Beowulf wants Hrothgar's lands and has come to conquer the Danes under the false pretense of helping to kill Grendel.
    B. Wulfgar has heard that Beowulf will need the help of the Danes to help hold his own borderlands, so he believes Beowulf has come in hopes of an exchange.
    C. According to Wulfgar, Beowulf wants to improve relations with the Danes in hopes of trading goods between the two lands.
    D. According to Wulfgar, God has sent Beowulf on his mission to help the Danes defeat Grendel.

16. Describe Beowulf's boasts upon meeting Hrothgar, King of the Danes.
    A. Beowulf boasts that he has more than twice the lands of Hrothgar.
    B. Beowulf greets Hrothgar by regaling him with stories of his great strength and prior exploits. Beowulf drove five giants into chains and chased them from the earth, and has hunted monsters out of the ocean.
    C. Beowulf greets Hrothgar formally and then proceeds to bore him with boasts of his army's great battles and victories. This, of course, is exactly the wrong thing to say to Hrothgar, who has recently come home victorious, himself.
    D. Beowulf was taken aback by the greeting he received at the Danish shore, and when he finally met with Hrothgar, he boasted that guests in Geatland are treated with a more hospitable welcome.

17. What one request does Beowulf make of Hrothgar?
    A. Beowulf asks for Hrothgar's help in Geatland in return for his help with Grendel.
    B. Beowulf asks Hrothgar to allow him and his men alone to drive Grendel from Herot.
    C. Beowulf asks Hrothgar to accompany him on his search for Grendel.
    D. Beowulf asks Hrothgar to give his men provisions for the search for Grendel.

18. If Beowulf loses the battle with Grendel, what are his instructions for after his death?
    A. He asks that his body would be sent out to sea and burned.
    B. Beowulf instructs Hrothgar to see that his soldiers are returned safely to Geatland to tell the tale of the battle and his death, so everyone there would know he died courageously and with honor in battle.
    C. Beowulf tells Hrothgar that if Grendel defeats him, the Danish king should send the mail of his armor to Higlac, and return the inheritance he had from Hrethel.
    D. Beowulf asks Hrothgar to seek revenge for his death.

Beowulf Multiple Choice Questions page 6
Prologue-Chapter 13

19. How did Hrothgar become king? What is his past relationship to the Geats?
    A. Hrothgar's father, the king, was killed by Grendel. Hrothgar's family had lost Geatland in battle several generations prior to this story.
    B. Hrothgar's older brother, Hergar, was king and died, making Hrothgar king. Hrothgar worked with Beowulf's father, Edgetho, to secure an earlier peace.
    C. When the king was killed by Grendel, there was no rightful successor to the throne. Because of his heroic deeds, bravery, and superior leadership, Hrothgar was given the throne by the Council of Danes. He was born in Geatland but had left home for adventure when he was a very young man.
    D. Hrothgar's father, Herot, died, leaving the throne to Hrothgar. Hrothgar had been going frequently to Geatland on hunting trips, and was most welcomed there.

20. What is the purpose of the feast that Hrothgar hosts in Beowulf's honor?
    A. The feast is to celebrate the union of the two lands.
    B. The feast is to honor Beowulf's past bravery, courage, and heroism.
    C. The feast is to honor Beowulf and his men before they head off to face Grendel.
    D. Hrothgar hosts the feast knowing Beowulf will be boastful and perhaps reveal his *real* reasons for coming to help the Danes.

21. Identify Unferth. Why does he seem to be perplexed by Beowulf's stories? How does he address Beowulf?
    A. Unferth is Hrothgar's brother who has just returned from a glorious victory. He is impressed by Beowulf's stories and brave deeds and addresses him as "Sir."
    B. Unferth is a soldier from Geatland. He is perplexed by Beowulf's stories because he was with Beowulf on most of the escapades, and Beowulf is clearly lying–distorting the truth to almost unrecognizable proportions. He addresses Beowulf as "My Lord."
    C. Unferth is a Danish nobleman who is angry that any warrior anywhere has achieved greater glory than he has. Unferth calls Beowulf a "boastful fool."
    D. Unferth is Hrothgar's servant. He is perplexed by the greatness of the tales Beowulf tells and addresses Beowulf as "master."

22. Describe Unferth's tale of the swimming competition between Brecca and Beowulf.
    A. The competition lasted four days and ended when Brecca encountered a sea monster. He battled the creature bravely, but lost. Beowulf swam on, won the competition, and told of Brecca's noble death.
    B. Brecca challenged Beowulf to a swimming competition to determine which of the two was the most fit. They swam for seven days and Beowulf, as expected, won.
    C. The swimming competition lasted seven hours. Brecca won with the help of the gods.
    D. Unferth tells the story of a swimming competition between Beowulf and Brecca that lasted for seven long nights and ended with the sea carrying Brecca home to victory—not far from the shores of his native Norway.

Beowulf Multiple Choice Questions page 7
Prologue-Chapter 13

23. What is Beowulf's response to Unferth's tale of the swimming competition?
    A. Beowulf can't believe Unferth has completely distorted the truth. He challenges Unferth to prove his story or duel with him.
    B. Beowulf recounts that he swam side by side with Brecca for five nights until a storm carried him away where he was attacked by sea monsters. He killed nine monsters before washing up on a Finnish beach.
    C. Beowulf thanks Unferth for such a wonderful account of the event and invites him to join him for dinner.
    D. Beowulf disputes Unferth's claim that Brecca was attacked by sea monsters. He says the truth is that Brecca got caught in a whirlpool and was too weak to swim out of it. The sea returned him to shore.

24. Beowulf continues with his story, countering Unferth's tale. How does his tale end?
    A. Beowulf explains that he killed many monsters and challenged Unferth to find any man—Brecca included—who could match his bravery.
    B. Beowulf renounces the validity of the competition because the gods helped Brecca. He says he will challenge Brecca to another competition–a fair one.
    C. Beowulf tells how he saw Brecca climb onto one of the sea monsters and ride it to shore, which was clearly cheating.
    D. Beowulf says that he was wounded helping Brecca fight the sea monsters, and after the monsters were defeated, Brecca swam on left him to die at sea.

25. Describe Welthow.
    A. Welthow is frequently described as being "icy"–cold and distant and forbearing.
    B. Welthow is Hrothgar's "gold-ringed Queen." She is described as a noble woman who knows "what is right."
    C. Welthow is a tall and slender beauty, but she is terribly jealous.
    D. Welthow is short, fat, and ugly, but Hrothgar loves her anyway because she is such a warm and loving person.

26. What is Hrothgar's declaration to Beowulf at the end of Chapter 9?
    A. Hrothgar declares Beowulf to be the greatest warrior of all time and offers to give him any woman in his kingdom.
    B. Hrothgar tells Beowulf that he has to leave because the tales of his bravery are spreading among the people causing too much of an uprising.
    C. Hrothgar pledges his life-long friendship to Beowulf, declaring that "wheresoever you go, wheresoever I am, should you need help, my friend, I will be there."
    D. Hrothgar tells Beowulf that no one has ever been granted the access to Herot that he is granting to the Geat warrior. He tells Beowulf to make Herot his own.

Beowulf Multiple Choice Questions page 8
Prologue-Chapter 13

27. Beowulf and his men move into Herot for the night while Hrothgar sleeps peacefully. What is Beowulf's boast?
    A. Beowulf boasts that he will defeat Grendel with his bare hands.
    B. Beowulf boasts that he will one day rule Herot and the Danish lands.
    C. Beowulf boasts that he once killed fourteen monsters in one battle.
    D. Beowulf boasts that he once quaffed an entire barrel of mead.

28. What do Beowulf's men think of their chances against Grendel?
    A. The men believe that Grendel will flee at the first sight of their fierce countenances.
    B. The men believe they will never see their homeland again, that they will be defeated by Grendel.
    C. The men believe Beowulf will get the monster drunk, then chop its head off.
    D. The men believe Grendel will kill all of them except one, who will tell the tale of the monster's exploits.

29. How does Grendel respond when he comes to Herot? Describe his reaction to seeing the sleeping Geats.
    A. Grendel tears the hinges off the door at Herot and is thrilled at the sight of the sleeping Geats—expecting to fill his belly with their meat.
    B. Grendel tears the hinges off the door, apologizes and tries to put the door back.
    C. Grendel climbs in through the window, but takes off running upon smelling Beowulf and his band.
    D. Grendel tears the hinges off the door, struts up to the throne, places the crown on his head and sits down, daring anyone to challenge him.

30. What happens when Grendel reaches for Beowulf?
    A. Beowulf stabs Grendel with a spear and the Geats go home.
    B. Beowulf's men jump up and surround Grendel, allowing Beowuf and Grendel to fight.
    C. Beowulf grabs Grendel and begins a hand to hand battle with him.
    D. Grendel shakes Beowulf awake, and the two have a drinking contest to determine who is the stronger of the two.

31. Describe the struggle that ensues between Beowulf and Grendel.
    A. Grendel rends the boastful warrior tooth and nail, stopping only to pick his teeth.
    B. Beowulf's arm is torn off by Grendel, but he continues to fight, ignoring his wound.
    C. Neither of the combatants can gain advantage over the other, and the battle rages for three days before a victor emerges.
    D. Herot trembles as Beowulf and Grendel fight to the death. Beowulf's prowess causes Grendel to shriek in agonizing pain.

Beowulf Multiple Choice Questions page 9
Prologue-Chapter 13

32. What happens when Beowulf's men attack Grendel?
    A. The men's spear points melt upon touching Grendel, as though he were molten hot.
    B. Grendel bewitched the weapons of Beowulf's men; they are unable to hurt the monster.
    C. Beowulf shouts for them to get back, saying he has Grendel under control.
    D. The men cause such confusion that they end up fighting each other instead of Grendel.

33. At the conclusion of the battle between Beowulf and Grendel, what transpires?
    A. Grendel is no match for Beowulf, who rips the monster's arm from its socket and leaves Grendel mortally wounded, running back to his cave.
    B. Grendel bites off Beowulf's head, but chokes on his helmet.
    C. Grendel is killed in the great hall, and his body is placed at the foot of Hrothgar's throne.
    D. Grendel and Beowulf roll on the floor, and are both crushed by one of the doors to the great hall that Grendel ripped from its hinges.

34. On the morning following the battle, describe the reactions of Hrothgar's people.
    A. They held a festival in the Geat's honor.
    B. They rejoiced with no sense of remorse for the monster's suffering.
    C. They declared Grendel an endangered species and fined Beowulf heavily.
    D. They began to rebuild their hall and sent Beowulf's band on their way with little thanks.

35. Describe the lake into which Grendel vanished.
    A. The lake was so full of debris from the monster's thrashing that nothing could be seen.
    B. The lake was covered over in ice from the evil presence below its surface.
    C. The lake had been dried up, and a cave was visible at the bottom of the lake bed.
    D. The lake into which Grendel vanished was steaming and boiling with blood, and it was very wavy.

36. Who is Siegmund? Why is his story recounted?
    A. Siegmund is the Geat who became Grendel after being seduced by evil magic.
    B. Siegmund was an ancient king who had conquered the Danes and pillaged their kingdom.
    C. Siegmund was a legendary hero to the Danes. Tales of his exploits were passed down through generations. Beowulf's victory over Grendel was likened to Siegmund's great feats.
    D. Siegmund is one of Beowulf's veterans who has had similar exploits to those of his leader. He is a living legend among the Geats, second only to Beowulf himself.

Beowulf Multiple Choice Questions page 10
Chapters 14-25

1. Upon seeing Grendel's bloody arm winging high from the "gold-shining roof" of Herot, what is Hrothgar's proclamation?
   A. Hrothgar is so overjoyed at the sight of Grendel's amputated arm and its implications, he makes Beowulf his own son and vows to forever preserve the peace between their people.
   B. Hrothgar is angered because the monster's corrosive blood has eaten through the roof.
   C. Hrothgar promises one hundred gold pieces to Beowulf's band for each piece of the monster likewise returned.
   D. Hrothgar asks if he may join the brave warriors in their future exploits, and travel to the kingdom of the Geats to further his own glory.

2. Describe Unferth's reaction to seeing the arm of Grendel.
   A. He quivers with terror, believing for an instant that Grendel is climbing over the roof.
   B. Unferth vows to all present that he will find what has become of the rest of the beast.
   C. Upon seeing Grendel's arm, Unferth falls on his own sword, too shamed by his inability to fulfill his own boasts.
   D. Upon seeing Grendel's arm, Unferth stops bragging, and he grows quiet, silenced by Beowulf's bravery.

3. What were Hrothgar's gifts to Beowulf for removing the threat of Grendel?
   A. Hrothgar gives Beowulf half of his Kingdom, a chest of gold and ten horses.
   B. Hrothgar gives Beowulf the pick of his best warriors to join his band and all the treasure he can carry.
   C. For defeating Grendel, Beowulf is given a golden banner to commemorate his victory, a coat of mail, and an ancient sword.
   D. Hrothgar gives Beowulf a gem from his own crown to commemorate his defeat of Grendel, as well as fifty of the finest bows in his arsenal.

4. What gifts does Hrothgar give to Beowulf's men?
   A. Hrothgar gives Beowulf's men ancient armor and swords.
   B. Hrothgar gives Beowulf's men their pick of the horses in his stables.
   C. Hrothgar gives Beowulf's men cloth of gold tunics and gold hilted daggers.
   D. Hrothgar gives Beowulf's men food and supplies for their return voyage.

5. How were the bodies of the dead disposed of in Anglo-Saxon times?
   A. In Anglo-Saxon times, the bodies of dead soldiers were placed in small pyramids.
   B. In Anglo-Saxon times, the bodies of dead soldiers were placed in giant burial mounds.
   C. In Anglo-Saxon times, the bodies of dead soldiers were buried as they are today.
   D. In Anglo-Saxon times, the bodies of dead soldiers were burned on a funeral pyre.

Beowulf Multiple Choice Questions page 11
Chapters 14-25

6. Who are the two sons of Hrothgar and Welthow? Why are they permitted at the victory feast?
    A. Henrich and Helmut are the sons of Hrothgar and Welthow. They are permitted at the victory feast because they have defeated monsters of their own.
    B. Herbert and Henry are the sons of Hrothgar and Welthow. They are permitted at the feast because they bought tickets.
    C. Hrethric and Hrothmund are the sons of Hrothgar and Welthow. They are permitted at the feast because they are the guests of Beowulf.
    D. Hans and Hobbes are the sons of Hrothgar and Welthow. They are permitted at the feast because they are hosting it in Beowulf's honor.

7. What gifts does Welthow give to Beowulf at the feast? What are her words to Beowulf about her sons?
    A. Welthow gives Beowulf a mail shirt, golden armbands, and "the most beautiful necklace known to men." She asks Beowulf to lend her two sons his wise and gentle heart.
    B. Welthow gives Beowulf a magic ring which makes him invisible. She asks Beowulf to spy on her sons for her.
    C. Welthow gives Beowulf a silver helmet, a leather saddle, and "the most valuable bangle in the Danish kingdom." She asks Beowulf to lend her two sons his keen strategic mind and strong arm as their general.
    D. Welthow gives Beowulf a silk shirt, copper bracers, and "the most wonderful scabbard known to swords." She asks Beowulf to lend her two sons his knowledge of blades and teach them to fight.

8. Why did the Danes sleep with their armor on?
    A. Sleeping in their armor helped keep lice and fleas off.
    B. It was the custom of the Danes to be ready for war.
    C. The Danes were afraid of being killed in their sleep by an invading enemy.
    D. The Danes made the most comfortable armor in the world.

9. How long had Grendel's mother dwelt in the cold, subterranean lake?
    A. Grendel's mother had lived in the lake since Nessie moved to Scotland.
    B. Grendel's mother had lived in the lake since the Roman Empire collapsed.
    C. Grendel's mother had lived in the lake since the birth of Thor.
    D. Grendel's mother had lived in the lake since Cain killed his brother Abel.

Beowulf Multiple Choice Questions page 12
Chapters 14-25

10. What is Grendel's mother's motive in coming to Herot?
    A. Grendel's mother comes to Herot seeking directions to Gaul.
    B. Grendel's mother comes to Herot seeking revenge for the loss of her son.
    C. Grendel's mother comes to Herot seeking humans to eat, having heard of them from her son.
    D. Grendel's mother comes to Herot seeking the blood of Unferth.

11. Whom does she snatch?
    A. Grendel's mother snatches Hrothgar's closest friend, Esher.
    B. Grendel's mother snatches Hrothgar's son, Hrethric.
    C. Grendel's mother snatches Sigemund.
    D. Grendel's mother snatches Unferth.

12. What individuals had witnessed the two fiends prior to the time of the attacks on Herot?
    A. Hrothgar's two sons had seen the pair lurking in the forest near Herot.
    B. One of Beowulf's men glimpsed the creatures shortly after the band put to shore in Denmark.
    C. The watchmen on the shore see the two creatures as Beowulf's band headed for the mead hall.
    D. The peasants in the field had witnessed Grendel and his mother lurking in the darkness prior to the attacks.

13. Describe the location of the place where Grendel lived with his mother.
    A. Grendel and his mother lived beneath a lake covered with algae and weeds. The lake seethed with filth and refuse, and it was rumored to be a gateway to hell.
    B. Grendel and his mother lived beneath a glacier, frozen solid except for a small hole which allowed the monsters to pass.
    C. Grendel and his mother lived beneath a lake covered with frozen spray. The lake burned "like a torch," and it was a lake rumored to be bottomless.
    D. Grendel and his mother lived beneath a mountain covered in briars and thorns. The mountain was rumored to have a system of caves hundreds of miles deep.

14. According to Beowulf, —what is the only thing that survives death?
    A. The only thing that survives death, according to Beowulf, is wealth.
    B. The only thing that survives death, according to Beowulf, is glory and fame.
    C. The only thing that survives death, according to Beowulf, is love.
    D. The only thing that survives death, according to Beowulf is a man's fighting spirit.

Beowulf Multiple Choice Questions page 13
Chapters 14-25

15. What do Hrothgar's men discover on their search for Grendel's mother?
    A. Hrothgar's men find the bloody head of Esher on their way to search for Grendel's mother.
    B. Hrothgar's men discover the armless body of Grendel.
    C. Hrothgar's men discover the burned out cottages of some peasants that Grendel's mother had killed in her flight from Herot.
    D. Hrothgar's men find the treasure Grendel had been hoarding in a tree stump.

16. Describe the lake that serves as the entrance to Grendel's mother's cave.
    A. The lake was clear blue snowmelt, and it was possible to see all the way to the cave at the bottom.
    B. The frozen lake had only a small hole in the ice, through which the seething water below shot high into the air.
    C. The blood red lake was thick with the vile stuff of Grendel's veins.
    D. The boiling lake was crawling with sea serpents.

17. What equipment does Beowulf adorn as he goes in pursuit of Grendel's mother? How is this different from what he wore in his battle with Grendel?
    A. Beowulf adorned only a small knife and a wool shirt. Beowulf was in full armor when he battled Grendel.
    B. Beowulf adorned armor, chain mail, Hrothgar's helmet, and Unferth's sword. Beowulf wore no armor in his battle with Grendel.
    C. Beowulf adorned scale-mail armor and two short swords. Beowulf wore plate armor in his battle with Grendel.
    D. Beowulf adorned the invisibility ring given to him by Welthow. In his battle with Grendel he wore no armor.

18. What is the significance of the sword, Hrunting?
    A. Hrunting is the sword given to Beowulf by Unferth. It has a shining blade and was hardened in blood.
    B. Hrunting is the sword which Hrothgar's fathers had passed down for a dozen generations.
    C. Hrunting is the sword which killed Grendel's father.
    D. Hrunting is the sword given to Hrothgar by a Finnish king. It has a gleaming blade and was hardened in water from Loki's drinking bowl.

Beowulf Multiple Choice Questions page 14
Chapters 14-25

19. Describe the encounter Beowulf has with Grendel's mother. How effective were his weapons?
    A. After Beowulf swims through the lake to her cave, his weapons quickly dispatch Grendel's mother. Beowulf's chain mail gets caught on a sunken branch and he almost drowns.
    B. After Beowulf swims through the lake for hours, his weapons began to glow blue, indicating he was close. Inside the cave, Beowulf's weapons work adequately, but only his chain mail stops him from being slain by Grendel's mother.
    C. After Beowulf swims through the lake to her cave, his weapons were useless against Grendel's mother, so he uses one of the sea-serpents from outside the cave to strangle her.
    D. After Beowulf swims for hours through the lake to her cave, his weapons were useless against Grendel's mother so he engages in hand-to-hand combat with her. She almost succeeded in stabbing Beowulf but his chain mail saved him.

20. How does Beowulf eventually slay Grendel's mother?
    A. Beowulf discovers a sword hanging on the wall of the cave and slices her neck through.
    B. Beowulf breaks Grendel's mother's neck with his bare hands, slaying her in a similar manner to her son.
    C. Beowulf discovers an old shield on the wall with which he bashes her over the head.
    D. Beowulf uses a serpent from outside the cave to poison Grendel's mother.

21. What does Beowulf do with the body of Grendel that he finds lying in the corner of the lair?
    A. Beowulf places the body on a funeral pyre, giving a hero's burial to a worthy adversary.
    B. Beowulf has Grendel stuffed and mounted as a warning to all other monsters.
    C. After finding Grendel's body, Beowulf cuts his head off.
    D. After finding Grendel's body, Beowulf ties it to the saddle of his horse and drags it through the streets for all to see.

22. What is happening on the surface with Hrothgar's men while Beowulf is fighting under the lake?
    A. Hrothgar's men are throwing dice on the shore of the lake, hoping for Beowulf's return but knowing that there is nothing they can do.
    B. Hrothgar's men take to small boats and drop stones into the lake, hoping to aid Beowulf in his struggle by killing the serpents below.
    C. Hrothgar's men speak of their own exploits, unwilling to give any credit to Beowulf until he has proven that the beast below is dead.
    D. Hrothgar's men on the surface speak of Beowulf as a warrior who has died in battle. They have lost hope in his return.

Beowulf Multiple Choice Questions page 15
Chapters 14-25

23. What happens to the "magnificent sword"?
    A. The "magnificent sword" becomes a family heirloom in the halls of Hrothgar, and is passed from father to son for generations.
    B. Beowulf gives the "magnificent sword" to his father upon returning to his homeland.
    C. The "magnificent sword" melted.
    D. Beowulf threw the "magnificent sword" into the sea, saying that any weapon that had touched something so vile was of no use to any noble warrior.

24. What does Beowulf take with him as souvenirs of his victory over Grendel's mother?
    A. As souvenirs of his victory, Beowulf takes Grendel's head and the hilt of the "magnificent sword."
    B. As souvenirs of his victory, Beowulf takes several weapons off the walls of the cave. He also cuts off Grendel's other arm.
    C. As souvenirs of his victory, Beowulf takes Hrothgar's helmet and Unferth's sword.
    D. As souvenirs of his victory, Beowulf takes Grendel's mother's head and the tooth of a serpent.

25. What "trophy" does Beowulf give to Hrothgar as a symbol of his victory over the demons?
    A. Beowulf present's Hrothgar with Grendel's other arm as a symbol of his victory.
    B. Beowulf presents Hrothgar with Grendel's mother's head as a symbol of his victory.
    C. Beowulf presents Hrothgar with the hilt of the "magnificent sword" as a symbol of his victory.
    D. Beowulf presents Hrothgar with Grendel's head as a symbol of his victory.

26. To what does Beowulf attribute his victory over Grendel's mother in his audience with Hrothgar?
    A. Beowulf attributes his victory to his own prowess.
    B. Beowulf attributes his victory to God's grace.
    C. Beowulf attributes his victory to the efforts of Hrothgar's men.
    D. Beowulf attributes his victory to the weakness of the monster.

Beowulf Multiple Choice Questions page 16
Chapters 13-25

27. Describe Hrothgar's reaction to what is written on the hilt of the sword. What is it?
    A. Hrothgar stares in contempt at the hilt of the sword that was forged by one of the people of Gaul, who are his mortal enemies. It is inscribed with tales of glorious victories over enemies that Hroghtar himself had defeated.
    B. Hrothgar gazes with wonder at the hilt of this sword that was forged by one of his own people long ago. On it is inscribed his entire family lineage up to his great, great grandfather.
    C. Hroghtar stares in amazement at the hilt of this sword that was forged by the gods to do battle with the ice giants in ancient times. The true name of the chief god is inscribed, as are the names of the lesser gods.
    D. Hrothgar stares in amazement at the hilt of this sword that was forged by giants and monsters. Its original owner's name is inscribed, as are stories of ancient wars between good and evil.

28. What has Hrothgar to say of the role of pride for a leader?
    A. Hrothgar cautions Beowulf against excessive pride and to realize that all glory is owed to God.
    B. Hrothgar cautions Beowulf to give due credit to those subordinates who help a leader on his path.
    C. Hrothgar tells Beowulf that he has every right to be proud of his accomplishments and any leader of his caliber can not boast overmuch.
    D. Hrothgar tells Beowulf that glory is fleeting and that he should not dwell on past deeds, however valorous they may be.

29. Before Beowulf and his men set sail on their return home, Unferth approaches Beowulf and offers him a gift. What is it? Explain its significance.
    A. Unferth gives Beowulf the gift of his helmet. This is the helmet that Unferth had boasted of earlier in his encounter with Beowulf.
    B. Unferth gives Beowulf the gift of his ring, as a token of honor passed from one lesser warrior to one greater.
    C. Unferth gives Beowulf the gift of his sword, Hrunting. This is the sword Unferth had boasted of earlier in his verbal bantering with Beowulf.
    D. Unferth gives Beowulf the gift of his servitude, pledging to follow the great warrior until his own quest called him.

Beowulf Multiple Choice Questions page 17
Chapters 26-35

1. What is Beowulf's vow to the Danes prior to his departure?
    A. Beowulf tells the king of the Danes that if he ever hears again that they are threatened; he will come to their aid.
    B. Beowulf tells the Danes that if ever again he hears they are threatened, he will send an army to aid them, but cannot return himself.
    C. Beowulf tells the Danes that if he ever hears again that they are threatened, he will not aid them.
    D. Beowulf vows that he and his men will always be there to support the Danes, as long as his King gives him leave.

2. Describe Hrothgar's final words to Beowulf. What realization does the old king make?
    A. Hrothgar tells Beowulf that the peace Beowulf has wrought will last as long as Beowulf offers his protection to the Danes. Hrothgar realizes that he is likely to die before the peace ends.
    B. Hrothgar tells Beowulf that the peace that he has brought to the Danes will last as long as Hrothgar lives and that the Geats and Danes shall always be friends. Hrothgar realizes, however, that he is likely never to see Beowulf again.
    C. Hrothgar tells Beowulf that he will always come to the aid of the Geats, and never fail to fulfill any request of Beowulf's. Hrothgar realizes that Beowulf will not take advantage of his generous oath.
    D. Hrothgar tells Beowulf that neither he nor his sons will ever make war on the Geats. Hrothgar realizes that Beowulf may not speak for his king and guarantee his own kingdom's safety.

3. Describe Higlac's queen. How is she received by the Geats?
    A. Higd was Higlac's wife from a political marriage. She was the daughter of the ruler of a neighboring kingdom. She is not well liked by the Geats.
    B. Higd was Higlac's wife, taken from an unknown people in a raid. She is cunning and witty, and is regarded with suspicion by the Geats.
    C. Higd was Higlac's first wife but he was not her first husband. She was queen before Higlac conquered the kingdom. When he slew her husband, he took her as his bride. The Geats regard her with a mix of suspicion and pity.
    D. Higd was Higlac's young wife who was wise and knowing beyond her years. She is highly received by the Geats.

Beowulf Multiple Choice Questions page 18
Chapters 26-35

4. Describe Beowulf's account of his adventures that he relates to his king, Higlac.
   A. Bewoulf tells his king, Higlac, that the Danes were sure to be weakened and threatened with invasion if he had not come to their aid.
   B. Beowulf tells his king of the battles he fought with the two monsters and that he thinks there might be similar creatures afflicting Higlac's own kingdom.
   C. Beowulf tells his king, Higlac, that he saved the Danes from certain slaughter and that he was received as a son by Hrothgar.
   D. Beowulf tells his king of the valor of his men in helping him defeat the beasts. He portrays them as the true saviors of the Danes.

5. Why might Ingeld and his followers be angry at seeing Beowulf's ancestral armor and weapons?
   A. Beowulf's ancestral armor and weapons are of much higher quality than those of Ingeld.
   B. Ingeld suggests that Beowulf's ancestral armor was involved in the slaying of Danes generations before.
   C. Ingeld sees symbols on Beowulf's ancestral armor that signify evil in his religion. He feels that Beowulf's ancestral armor is an affront to his god.
   D. Beowulf's ancestral armor was made by a Dane, and Ingeld thinks it was stolen long ago from his kingdom.

6. Why is this chapter devoted to the re-telling of the tale of Beowulf's victories over Grendel and his mother?
   A. The re-telling of this tale served as a mnemonic device for oral storytellers before the tale was finally written down.
   B. Higlac demanded this recapitulation from Beowulf upon his return.
   C. The re-telling of the tale boosted the morale of Beowulf's men after their long sea voyage back to their home.
   D. The re-telling of the victories that Beowulf experienced over Grendel and his mother serve to immortalize Beowulf's fame through the repetition of these tales of glory.

7. How does Higlac reward Beowulf for his feats?
   A. Higlac rewards Beowulf by giving him Beowulf's grandfather's ancestral sword, in addition to seven thousand hides of land.
   B. Higlac rewards Beowulf with five hundred men to command and ten thousand gold pieces to finance his campaign.
   C. Higlac gives Beowulf a suit of chain mail armor and the title of thane.
   D. Higlac gives Beowulf a chest of jewels and seven hundred hides of land.

Beowulf Multiple Choice Questions page 19
Chapters 26-35

8. Who is king after Higlac? How does he die?
    A. Higlac's son, Volf, succeeds him to the throne. He is killed by an assassin from another kingdon.
    B. Higlac's daughter, Ceclynd succeeds him to the throne, after he dies of old age.
    C. Higlac's son, Herdred, succeeds him to the throne. He is killed in a battle with the Swedes.
    D. Hrothgar succeeds him to the throne after conquering the Geats in battle. Higlac is executed by Hrothgar.

9. What large event happens fifty years into Beowulf's reign?
    A. After fifty years on the throne, Beowulf is called back to Denmark to face another relative of Grendel.
    B. After fifty years on the throne, Beowulf is faced with an awakening dragon that has come to terrorize the Geats.
    C. After fifty years on the throne, Beowulf's men rebel and fight him for the kingship.
    D. After fifty years on the throne, Beowulf takes a small band back to Denmark, answering the call of Hrothgar's grandson, who is now king.

10. Why did the slave steal from the dragon? What was his motivation?
    A. The slave was motivated solely by greed. He desired to be richer than his master.
    B. The slave stole from the dragon hoping to curry favor with his master by leading him to the hoard.
    C. The slave stole from the dragon, not from desire but from need.
    D. The slave was sent to the dragon by his master and was told to steal.

11. How did the dragon's tower come to have so many riches?
    A. The dragon had collected the treasure from all across the countryside.
    B. The treasure guarded by the dragon was left there by the gods to lure greedy men to their doom at the hands of the dragon.
    C. The dragon had uprooted the burial mound of a king and brought its contents to the tower to better guard them.
    D. The treasure guarded by the dragon came from the last survivor of a noble race.

12. Describe how the dragon discovered the riches.
    A. The dragon made a deal with the great warrior to guard his treasure after the warrior had died.
    B. After the great warrior died, a dragon seeking shelter found the treasure and stayed to guard it.
    C. The dragon pillaged the treasure from the stronghold of a far off country and had brought it to the land of the Geats to protect it from being recovered.
    D. The dragon came upon the treasure in the time of a kingdom long since forgotten to Geats and decided to stay and protect it through the ages.

Beowulf Multiple Choice Questions page 20
Chapters 26-35

13. What does Beowulf think has brought on the wrath of the dragon?
    A. Beowulf, having been appraised of the slave's discovering the dragon, blamed him for it's rampage over the countryside.
    B. Beowulf thinks that the dragon is a last test sent to him by God to ensure his glory.
    C. Beowulf felt that because he as a king had broken God's law, the dragon wreaked his wrath upon the Geats.
    D. Beowulf felt that because he had been so successful, fate was trying to undo him, and the dragon was fate's instrument.

14. Describe the dragon's "hidden home."
    A. The dragon's "hidden home" was enclosed by giant stones set deep in the ground with water beating on rocks close by.
    B. The dragon's "hidden home" was enclosed by giant trees and impassible brush with a river leading to a waterfall on one side.
    C. The dragon's "hidden home" was a cave at the mouth of a fjord with high cliffs on all sides.
    D. The dragon's "hidden home" was an ancient crumbling castle long since abandoned by men.

15. Why does Beowulf again recount the glory of his day's past before taking on a battle with the dragon?
    A. Beowulf recounts his history to remind himself of all his valorous deeds in an attempt to convince himself that he will survive taking on this foe.
    B. Beowulf reviews his accomplishments as if balancing his life on scales, feeling that the different set of scales before him might be the end.
    C. Beowulf reviews his accomplishments prior to the battle with the dragon, as if to underscore his worthiness to take on this foe.
    D. Beowulf recounts his accomplishments as if to say, in his usual boastful way, that for one who had done all that he had, this dragon was just a footnote.

16. How does Beowulf feel about his upcoming battle against the dragon?
    A. Beowulf feels no fear of the dragon. He yearns for the battle to commence, that he might increase his glory.
    B. Beowulf's mind was clouded with anger at what the dragon had done to his Geats. He was determined to exact revenge.
    C. Beowulf was awestruck by the magnificent creature before him. He could not see himself killing so magnificent a beast.
    D. Beowulf's heart was heavy, and he had a sense of doom prior to meeting the dragon in battle.

Beowulf Multiple Choice Questions page 21
Chapters 26-35

17. Why does Beowulf announce that he is going to fight the dragon alone?
    A. Beowulf fears for the safety of his Geats against the wrath of such a savage creature as a dragon.
    B. Beowulf tells the Geats that in every battle his place was in the front, alone, and so shall it be against the dragon.
    C. Beowulf cannot let himself merely command another to slay the creature, for he still craved glory as he had in his youth.
    D. Beowulf saw the fear on the faces of his warriors, and knew that no other would step forward to face the dragon.

18. What do Beowulf's men do as he is taking on the dragon?
    A. Beowulf's followers hid themselves in the mead hall while Beowulf took on the dragon.
    B. Beowulf's men slowly began to join their lord in the fight against the dragon, once they saw he was not immediately slain.
    C. Beowulf's followers ran for their lives as their leader took on the dragon.
    D. Beowulf's followers stood by their king while he battled the dragon.

Beowulf Multiple Choice Questions page 22
Chapters 36-43

1. Identify: Wiglaf.
   A. Wiglaf was a brave soldier who came to the assistance of Beowulf.
   B. Wiglaf was the narrator of Beowulf.
   C. Wiglaf was Beowulf's son.
   D. Wiglaf was Beowulf's second in command.

2. What prior battle experience has Wiglaf experienced?
   A. Wiglaf was a seasoned veteran of several wars.
   B. Wiglaf was an unseasoned warrior but a good soldier.
   C. Wiglaf had only participated in a few skirmishes.
   D. Wiglaf was a poor soldier, fit only for the meanest of duties.

3. Describe the effectiveness of Beowulf's sword, Nagling.
   A. Beowulf's sword bends on the dragon's hide.
   B. Beowulf's sword is destroyed by the dragon.
   C. Beowulf's sword pierces the dragon's hide but does no apparent damage.
   D. Beowulf's sword dispatches the dragon easily, cutting its hide as though it were cloth.

4. Describe how Beowulf and Wiglaf join forces to slay the dragon.
   A. Beowulf struck at the dragon's head with a spear while Wiglaf slit its belly open.
   B. Wiglaf threw stones at the dragon to distract it long enough for Beowulf to cut off its head.
   C. Wiglaf chopped off pieces of the dragon's tail while Beowulf cut at its wings. When the beast could no longer move, they both plunged their swords into its back.
   D. Wiglaf struck at the dragon's lower half while Beowulf engaged the fire of the dragon. While Wiglaf distracted the dragon, Beowulf split the beast in two.

5. What is Beowulf's dying wish?
   A. Before he dies, Beowulf wishes to see the dragon's treasure—what he has died for.
   B. Before he dies, Beowulf asks his Geats to never make war on the Danes.
   C. Before he dies, Beowulf wishes that Wiglaf make his funeral pyre from the body of the dragon.
   D. Before he dies, Beowulf asks that the men who fled be forgiven their cowardice.

6. How does Beowulf react when he sees the treasure?
   A. Beowulf is angered that he gave his life for so little return.
   B. Beowulf thanks Wiglaf for coming to his aid, and giving him the opportunity to see what his death had bought.
   C. Beowulf prays to God, thanking him for opportunity to bring this treasure to his people.
   D. Beowulf just smiles, content in the cloak of glory that has woven itself about his life.

Beowulf Multiple Choice Questions page 23
Chapters 36-43

7. What are his funeral instructions? Why?
   A. Beowulf asks to be burnt in a boat, because it is the tradition of his ancestors.
   B. Beowulf asks that the Geats build him a tall tomb so that all sailors who pass by on the sea will know that a great man is buried there.
   C. Beowulf asks that he be buried in secret, so that he may become a legend, rather than a man whose grave may be visited.
   D. Beowulf instructs that he and he dragon be burned together, as they died together.

8. After both Beowulf and the dragon are slain, how do Beowulf's followers behave? What does Wiglaf say to them?
   A. Beowulf's followers immediately fall on the treasure. Wiglaf chastens them for their cowardice in the face of danger.
   B. Upon hearing that their lord and the dragon are both slain, the people spend days lamenting the loss of their great king.
   C. After the danger has past, Beowulf's cowardly followers come out of hiding. Wiglaf angrily tells them that they are a disgrace to their people.
   D. Wiglaf calls out Beowulf's followers, and forgives them for running from the dragon.

9. According to the messenger who announces Beowulf's death to his people, what might the Geats expect now from their enemies?
   A. The messenger tells the Geats that they can expect bitter quarrels now with the Franks and the Frisians once word reaches them of Beowulf's death.
   B. The messenger tells the Geats that they can expect constant skirmishes from their enemies.
   C. The messenger warns the Geats of an invading army coming from the north, their spies having witnessed the battle.
   D. The messenger tells the Geats to expect embassies from their enemies to take the measure of the new king.

10. Wiglaf decrees that all the treasure should be burned. What is his reason for this?
    A. Wiglaf tells the people that Beowulf wished the treasure to be so destroyed.
    B. Wiglaf tells the people that the treasure will attract unwanted attention from their enemies.
    C. Wiglaf tells the people that the treasure would cause internal conflicts and divide the kingdom.
    D. Wiglaf tells the people that no one living should enjoy the jewels; they are not worthy.

Beowulf Multiple Choice Questions page 24
Chapters 36-43

11. What role does fate play in Beowulf's demise, according to Wiglaf?
    A. Wiglaf believes that there was no other way so great a man as Beowulf could have died.
    B. Wiglaf tells the people that fate had the dragon in store for Beowulf. It was "meant to be."
    C. Wiglaf believed that fate had no part in Beowulf's death, and that Beowulf, great as he was, was no match for a dragon.
    D. Wiglaf tells the people that fate chose him to lead after Beowulf's death.

12. What do the Geats do with the dragon's body?
    A. The Geats hold a great feast and serve the dragon in honor of their fallen king.
    B. The dragon is burnt on the pyre below Beowulf.
    C. The Geats make armor from the skin of the dragon, and shields from its bones.
    D. The Geats rolled the dragon's body off the cliff and into the sea.

13. Describe Beowulf's funeral pyre.
    A. Beowulf's is called the harbinger of funeral pyres, for it lit the flames of war for the Geats.
    B. Beowulf's is called the greatest of funeral pyres, heaven was said to have swallowed the smoke of his pyre.
    C. Beowulf's is called the immortal funeral pyre, it burned for days on end before the rain could extinguish it.
    D. Beowulf's funeral pyre was so bright that ships used it as a lighthouse for a night.

14. What is the role of the twelve horsemen who surround Beowulf's monument?
    A. The twelve Geat horsemen who rode around Beowulf's monument told of his deeds and of the greatness of his glory so that all would remember the great Geat warrior.
    B. The twelve horsemen are Beowulf's vanguard into the next life.
    C. The twelve Geat horsemen were guards, keeping the curious treasure seekers away from the tomb of the great warrior.
    D. The twelve Geat horsemen were messengers sent to the twelve nearest kingdoms, bearing the tale of Beowulf's life.

ANSWER KEY - MULTIPLE CHOICE STUDY/QUIZ QUESTIONS
Beowulf

INTRO	PROLOGUE-CHAPTER 13	CHAPTERS 14-25	CHAPTERS 26-35	CHAPTERS 36-43
1 C	1 C	1 A	1 A	1 A
2 B	2 B	2 D	2 B	2 B
3 A	3 A	3 C	3 D	3 B
4 D	4 B	4 A	4 C	4 D
	5 A	5 D	5 B	5 B
	6 C	6 C	6 D	6 C
	7 C	7 A	7 A	7 B
	8 D	8 B	8 C	8 C
	9 A	9 D	9 B	9 A
	10 C	10 B	10 C	10 D
	11 C	11 A	11 D	11 B
	12 A	12 D	12 B	12 D
	13 D	13 C	13 C	13 B
	14 A	14 B	14 A	14 A
	15 D	15 A	15 C	
	16 B	16 D	16 D	
	17 B	17 B	17 B	
	18 C	18 A	18 C	
	19 B	19 D		
	20 C	20 A		
	21 C	21 C		
	22 D	22 D		
	23 B	23 C		
	24 A	24 A		
	25 B	25 D		
	26 D	26 B		
	27 A	27 D		
	28 B	28 A		
	29 A	29 C		
	30 C			
	31 D			
	32 B			
	33 A			
	34 B			
	35 D			
	36 C			

PREREADING VOCABULARY WORKSHEETS

VOCABULARY - Introduction *Beowulf*

Part I: Using Prior Knowledge and Contextual Clues

Below are the sentences in which the vocabulary words appear in the text. Read the sentence. Use any clues you can find in the sentence combined with your prior knowledge, and write what you think the underlined words mean on the lines provided.

1. A single manuscript managed to survive Henry VIII's <u>dissolution</u> of the monasteries, and the destruction of their great libraries.

___

2. And this England of roughly the eighth century A.D., as reflected in social patterns <u>ascribed</u> to sixth-century Geats and Danes and Swedes, is rigidly feudal, highly civilized and highly violent, and rather newly Christian.

___

3. Much of the poem is <u>ruminative</u> rather than, as might be expected, more narrowly narrative.

___

4. The battle scene, <u>tripartite</u> now, is well worth waiting for; the point is that for the poet no battle is simply men hacking at each other (or at monsters of various descriptions).

___

5. They are people to be known about, to be <u>emulated</u>, but not blindly, not only because they are successful (death being the supreme product of their occupation).

___

6. None of his descriptive passages are autotelic; they are all purposeful, meant to <u>elucidate</u> or set the stage or accomplish a transition.

___

7. I have commented in my *Poems from the Old English*, on the gentleness and <u>solicitude</u> shown by Wiglaf.

___

Beowulf Vocabulary Worksheet for the Introduction Continued

Part II: Determining the Meaning
   Match the vocabulary words to their dictionary definitions

___ 1. dissolution   A. consisting of three parts
___ 2. ascribed   B. anxiety or concern
___ 3. ruminative   C. dispersal
___ 4. tripartite   D. meditative, pondering
___ 5. emulated   E. attributed, assigned
___ 6. elucidate   F. to rival with some degree of success
___ 7. solicitude   G. to make clear

Vocabulary – *Beowulf* Prologue through Chapter 13

Part I: Using Prior Knowledge and Contextual Clues
Below are the sentences in which the vocabulary words appear in the text. Read the sentence. Use any clues you can find in the sentence combined with your prior knowledge, and write what you think the underlined words mean in the space provided.

1. Forced to set him adrift, floating
   As far as the tide might run, they refused
   To give him less from their hoards of gold
   Than those who'd shipped him away, an orphan
   And a beggar, to cross the waves alone.

   _____

2. No one
   Waited for reparation from his plundering claws:

   _____

3. And sometimes they sacrificed to the old stone gods,
   Made heathen vows, hoping for Hell's support, the Devil's guidance in driving
   Their affliction off.

   _____

4. None
   Of the wise ones regretted his going, much
   As he was loved by the Geats: the omens were good,
   And they urged the adventure on.

   _____

5. The path he'd shown was paved, cobbled
   Like a Roman road.

   _____

6. I bought the end of Edgetho's
   Quarrel, sent his ancient treasures through the oceans
   Furrows to the Wulfings.

   _____

Vocabulary – *Beowulf* Prologue through Chapter 13 Continued

7. But he's learned that terror is his alone,
   Discovered he can come for your people with no
   Fear of <u>reprisal</u>; he's found no fighting here,
   But only food, only delight.

   _____

8. His mind was flooded with fear—but nothing
   Could take his <u>talons</u> and himself from that tight
   Hard grip.

   _____

9. That trip to
   Herot
   Was a miserable journey for the <u>writhing</u> monster!

   _____

10. In the darkness the horrible shrieks of pain
    And defeat, the tears torn out of Grendel's
    <u>Taut</u> throat, hell's captive caught in the arms
    Of him who of all men on earth
    Was the strongest.

Part II: Determining the Meaning
   Match the vocabulary words to their dictionary definitions

   _____ 1. hoards   A. tight
   _____ 2. reparation   B. pagan, non-Christian
   _____ 3. heathen   C. narrow, trench-like depressions
   _____ 4. omens   D. claws
   _____ 5. cobbled   E. a group or accumulation
   _____ 6. furrows   F. twisting and squirming
   _____ 7. reprisal   G. process of making amends
   _____ 8. talons   H. stones roughly placed together
   _____ 9. writhing   I. prophetic signs
   _____10. taut   J. retaliation

Vocabulary – *Beowulf* Chapters 14-25

Part I: Using Prior Knowledge and Contextual Clues
Below are the sentences in which the vocabulary words appear in the text. Read the sentence. Use any clues you can find in the sentence combined with your prior knowledge, and write what you think the underlined words mean in the space provided.

1. A funeral <u>pyre</u> was prepared, and gold
   Was brought; Hnaf's dead body was dressed
   For burning, and the others with him.

   _____

2. Then Hnaf's sister,
   Finn's sad wife, gave her son's body
   To be burned in that fire; the flames <u>charring</u>
   His uncle would consume both kinsmen at once.

   _____

3. His body, and his shining coat of mail,
   And that necklace, all lay for Franks to pluck,
   For <u>jackal</u> warriors to find when they walked
   Through
   The rows of corpses…

   _____

4. The savage fate
   <u>Decreed</u> for them hung dark and unknown, what
   Would follow after nightfall, when Hrothgar withdrew from the
   Hall…

   _____

5. He drew it
   From its <u>scabbard</u>, broke the chain on its hilt,
   And then, savage, new, angry
   And desperate, lifted it high over his head…

   _____

Vocabulary – *Beowulf* Chapters 14-25 Continued

6. Then he gave the golden sword <u>hilt</u>
   To Hrothgar, who held it in his wrinkled hands
   And stared at what giants had made, and monsters
   Owned…

   _____

7. And Hrothgar saw the <u>runic</u> letters
   Clearly carved in that shining hilt,
   Spelling its original owner's name…

   _____

8. Your
   Strength must <u>solace</u> your people,
   Now, and mine no longer.

Part II: Determining the Meaning
   Match the vocabulary words to their dictionary definitions.

   _____ 1. pyre   A. sheath or cover for a sword
   _____ 2. charring   B. comfort in sorrow
   _____ 3. jackal   C. burning
   _____ 4. decreed   D. an ancient, interlacing script
   _____ 5. scabbard   E. a pile of wood for burning dead bodies
   _____ 6. hilt   F. ordered by a judge
   _____ 7. runic   G. one who meanly serves the purpose of another
   _____ 8. solace   H. the handle of a sword or dagger

Vocabulary – *Beowulf* Chapters 26-35

Part I: Using Prior Knowledge and Contextual Clues
Below are the sentences in which the vocabulary words appear in the text. Read the sentence. Use any clues you can find in the sentence combined with your prior knowledge, and write what you think the underlined words mean in the space provided.

1. And then Beowulf left him, left Herot, walked
   Across the green in his golden armor,
   Exulting in the treasures heaped high in his arms.

   _____

2. Deck timbers creaked,
   And the wind billowing through the sail stretched
   From the mast, tied tight with ropes, did not hold
   Them.

   _____

3. She was Hareth's daughter, a noble queen
   With none of the niggardly ways of women
   With open hands.

   _____

4. I sought
   And found her, the horrible hag, fierce
   And wild; we fought, clutching and grasping…

   _____

5. Beowulf had brought his king
   Horses and treasure—as a man must,
   Not weaving nets of malice for his comrades,
   Preparing their death in the dark, with secret,
   Cunning tricks.

   _____

6. These hammered
   Helmets, worked with gold, will tarnish
   And crack; the hands that should clean and polish
   Them
   Are still forever.

   _____

Vocabulary – *Beowulf* Chapters 26-35 Continued

7. The Geats
Deserved revenge; Beowulf, their leader
And lord, began to plan it, ordered
A battle-shield shaped of iron, knowing that
Wood would be useless, that no <u>linden</u> shield
Could help him, protect him, in the flaming heat…

_____

8. The place
Where his son once dwelled,
Before death <u>compelled</u>
Him to journey away…

_____

Part II: Determining the Meaning
Match the vocabulary words to their dictionary definitions.

_____ 1. exulting   A. discoloration of metal
_____ 2. billowing   B. Rejoicing triumphantly
_____ 3. niggardly   C. forced
_____ 4. hag   D. stingy
_____ 5. malice   E. trees with heart-shaped leaves
_____ 6. tarnish   F. flowing, rising on the winds
_____ 7. linden   G. a repulsive old woman
_____ 8. compelled   H. evil intent

Vocabulary – *Beowulf* Chapters 36-43

Part I: Using Prior Knowledge and Contextual Clues
Below are the sentences in which the vocabulary words appear in the text. Read the sentence. Use any clues you can find in the sentence combined with your prior knowledge, and write what you think the underlined words mean in the space provided.

1. He meant to kill
   This monster himself, our mighty king,
   Fight this battle alone and <u>unaided</u>,
   As in the days when his strength and daring dazzled
   Men's eyes.

   _____

2. The sword
   Sank in; his hand was burned, but the shining
   Blade had done its work, the dragon's
   <u>Belching</u> flames began to flicker
   And die away.

   _____

3. He could feel something stirring, burning
   In his veins, a stinging <u>venom</u>, and knew
   The beast's fangs had left it.

   _____

4. He <u>groped</u> his way,
   A brave young warrior, and suddenly saw
   Piles of gleaming gold, precious
   Gems, scattered on the floor…

   _____

5. Beholding the treasure, he spoke <u>haltingly</u>:

   _____

6. Brave, but wise, he fled, sought safety
   Behind <u>earthen</u> walls.

   _____

Vocabulary – *Beowulf* Chapters 36-43 Continued

7. The Geats, who'd survived, who'd escaped him,
Calling
Threats and boasts at that <u>wretched</u> band
The whole night through.

Part II: Determining the Meaning
Match the vocabulary words to their dictionary definitions.

_____ 1. unaided
_____ 2. belching
_____ 3. venom
_____ 4. groped
_____ 5. haltingly
_____ 6. earthen
_____ 7. wretched

A. hesitatingly
B. unassisted
C. made of dirt
D. bursting with flame or smoke
E. poison
F. searched for blindly
G. miserable, pitiable

VOCABULARY ANSWER KEY *Beowulf*

Introduction

1. C
2. E
3. D
4. A
5. F
6. G
7. B

Prologue through Chapter 13

8. E
9. G
10. B
11. I
12. H
13. C
14. J
15. D
16. F
17. A

Chapters 14-25

18. E
19. C
20. G
21. F
22. A
23. H
24. D
25. B

Chapters 26-35

26. B
27. F
28. D
29. G
30. H
31. A
32. E
33. C

Chapters 36-43

34. B
35. D
36. E
37. F
38. A
39. C
40. G

DAILY LESSONS

LESSON ONE

Objectives
1. To introduce the theme of heroism and the quest for heroic ideals and adventures
2. To brainstorm about the traits common to heroic individuals
3. To distribute books and other related materials

NOTE: Prior to Lesson One you need to have assigned for students to bring to class a list of modern day heroes and a short (1-2 sentence) rationale for each selection. Encourage the students to bring in pictures of these heroes to class. Also, you should have an empty bulletin board with just background paper and the title: BEOWULF: INFLUENCING THE HEROES OF THE FUTURE.

Activity #1
Tell students to take out the names and the pictures they were assigned to bring to class. On prepared 2"x5" pre-cut strips of colored paper, ask students to write the names of their modern day heroes on the paper strips, using markers that you have on hand. When they have finished, ask each student to post his picture(s) and the corresponding colored name strips on the bulletin board and, as he does so, to explain to the class why he has selected that person as a modern day hero.

TRANSITION: Explain to the students that *Beowulf*, the book they are about to read, is a tale about heroism, and what qualities are common among heroes—both from the modern day and the past.

Activity #2
Have the students scrutinize the names and faces on the bulletin board, and then have them brainstorm aloud in class—by way of a class discussion—the traits common to the heroes listed on the board. Have the students copy this list into their notebooks for further comparison as *Beowulf* is examined in the days ahead.

Activity #3
Distribute the materials students will use in this unit. Explain in detail how students are to use these materials.

Study Guides Students should read the study guide questions for each reading assignment prior to beginning the reading assignment to get a feeling for what events and ideas are important in the section they are about to read. After reading the section, students will (as a class or individually) answer the questions to review the important events and ideas from that section of the book. Students should keep the study guides as study materials for the unit test.

Vocabulary Prior to reading a reading assignment, students will do vocabulary work related to the section of the book they are about to read. Following the completion of the reading of the book, there will be a vocabulary review of all the words used in the vocabulary assignments. Students should keep their vocabulary work as study materials for the unit test.

Reading Assignment Sheet   You need to fill in the reading assignment sheet to let students know by when their reading has to be completed. You can either write the assignment sheet up on a side blackboard or bulletin board and leave it there for students to see each day, or you can "ditto" copies for each student to have. In either case, you should advise students to become very familiar with the reading assignments so they know what is expected of them.

Extra Activities Center   The Unit Resource Materials portion of this LitPlan contains suggestions for an extra library of related books and articles in your classroom as well as crossword and word search puzzles. Make an extra activities center in your room where you will keep these materials for students to use. (Bring the books and articles in from the library and keep several copies of the puzzles on hand.) Explain to students that these materials are available for students to use when they finish reading assignments or other class work early.

Nonfiction Assignment Sheet   Explain to students that they each are to read at least one non-fiction piece from the in-class library at some time during the unit. Students will fill out a nonfiction assignment sheet after completing the reading to help you (the teacher) evaluate their reading experiences and to help the students think about and evaluate their own reading experiences.

Books   Each school has its own rules and regulations regarding student use of school books. Advise students of the procedures that are normal for your school. Preview the book. Look at the covers, frontmatter, and index. Glance through at some of the drawings.

LESSON TWO

Objectives
1. To introduce students to the genre of the literary epic
2. To provide a historical context for *Beowulf*
3. To preview the study questions for "Raffel's Introduction to Beowulf"
4. To familiarize students with the vocabulary from "The Introduction"

NOTE: Prior to the students' arrival in class, have written the following on the board or on an overhead projection screen:

FEATURES OF A LITERARY EPIC
1. It is a long narrative poem that reflects the values of the society that produced it.
2. The story began in the oral tradition and contains some element of historical accuracy.
3. It is written in a serious, elevated style.
4. The author is usually anonymous.
5. It deals with large issues of good versus evil.
6. It has a hero who is "larger than life"; stronger, braver, and more insightful than the average man.
7. The hero is on a quest wherein the fate of his tribe, his nation, or the entire human race rests on his shoulders.
8. Gods or other quasi-divine creatures come to the aid of one side and/or another.

Activity #1
Introduce the genre of the literary epic by discussing the "Features of an Epic" that you have displayed either on the board or on an overhead projector. In the interest of time, distribute a printed copy to each student. Discuss the epic features with the class and suggest that literary epics often translate into film versions and inspirations. Ask the class what films seem to have many of these same literary epic features. (Responses will vary. *The Lord of the Rings* Trilogy, the *Star Wars* series, and even the latest version of *Troy* all have epic features). Discuss why epic films appeal to us.

TRANSITION: Explain to the students that epics appeal to people who share a common value system, and that in order to understand Beowulf as a literary epic, it is important to comprehend "the world of the work"—what the historical context of the poem is.

Activity #2
Burton Raffel, the translator of this edition of the *Beowulf* epic, provides a very strong history of Anglo-Saxon life, values, and society, at the time that *Beowulf* was written. Preview the highlights of Raffel's introductory narrative by calling attention to the following important elements about *Beowulf*'s composition:

1. *Beowulf* survived the monastery fires set by Henry VIII in the 16th century in England.
2. It is the sole surviving manuscript from what was believed to have been a thriving literary form.
3. A single manuscript of *Beowulf* exists in the British Museum in London where it survived a fire in the 18th century.
4. It is an archaeological relic.
5. It is an aristocratic poem exclusively—concerned with issues of kingship
6. Traits valued and heralded by the Anglo-Saxons (and seen in *Beowulf*) included: courage, bravery, strength, loyalty and obedience to one's lord, generosity, willingness to engage in battle, and the quest for fame.
7. Beowulf originated as a pagan piece in the oral tradition.
8. Eighth century monks "Christianized" the piece, so it is an interesting hybrid of Christian and non-Christian elements.
9. Beowulf faces three large challenges. (Discuss the significance of the number "3" in the Christian tradition).
10. The poem begins with a "Song of Creation" celebrating the gifts bestowed by God—then quickly moves to the dark narration of the challenges Beowulf is about to meet.
11. The sharp and beautiful language of the poem can be attributed to the fact that it began in the oral tradition.

Activity #3

Tell students that they have the remainder of the class period to do the pre-reading work for "Raffel's Introduction to *Beowulf*" on pp ix-xxii; that is to do the vocabulary worksheet and preview the study questions for the Introduction.

LESSON THREE

Objectives
1. To review the study questions from "The Introduction by Burton Raffel"
2. To introduce students to literary devices to be aware of as they read the poetic text of *Beowulf*
3. To preview the study questions for The Prologue through Chapter 13
4. To familiarize students with the vocabulary from the Prologue through Chapter 13

Activity #1

Discuss the answers to the study questions for "The Introduction" in detail. Note: In advance of this activity consider assigning pairs of students to lead the discussions on a pre-assigned day. This will give them the opportunity to practice public speaking and leadership skills. The teacher should guide the discussion when appropriate and be sure to fill in any gaps the students leave.

Activity #2

Write the following literary terms on the board: *rhythm, alliteration, allegory,* and *kenning*. Ask students if they know the literary definitions for these terms, and to provide examples from their memory, if possible.

Define the terms on the board:

Rhythm – the metrical movement of the flow of words on a page, as in poetry, the pulse of the poetic lines

Alliteration – the repetition of the initial or the first consonant sound in a line of poetry

Allegory – a story told on two levels, one that is literal and one that seeks to teach a lesson or a moral

Kenning – a uniquely Anglo-Saxon literary device in which straightforward nouns are called by a poetic arrangement of words to embellish the effects of an orally transmitted narration (*e.g. "heaven's high arch" for "rainbow" or "whale road" for the "sea"*).

NOTE: Ask students to look for and to bring in concrete examples of these literary devices as they complete the night's reading

Activity #3

Give the students the remaining class time to preview the study questions and the vocabulary for the Prologue through Chapter 13 of *Beowulf*.

LESSON 4

Objectives

1. To review examples of the literary devices introduced in Lesson 3
2. To review the study questions from the Prologue through Chapter 13 of *Beowulf*
3. To have the students practice writing to inform by developing and organizing facts to convey information

Activity #1

Review with the students the following literary terms and devices as introduced in Lesson 3: *rhythm, alliteration, allegory,* and *kenning*. Ask student to use the text (page and line numbers) to provide examples of these terms and devices.

Activity #2

Discuss the answers to the study questions from the Prologue through Chapter 13. Ideally, it would be advantageous for pairs of students who have been pre-assigned these chapters to lead the discussions. The teacher should guide the discussion when appropriate and fill in any gaps left by the students.

Activity #3

Distribute Writing Assignment #1 and discuss the directions in detail. Give students the remainder of the class period to work on this assignment.

WRITING ASSIGNMENT #1 - *Beowulf*

PROMPT
Although you have read thus far only the first part of this tripartite epic, *Beowulf's* epic qualities are already self-evident. Using examples and quotations from the text to support your thesis, explain the ways in which *Beowulf* manifests the features of a literary epic.

PREWRITING
The first thing you need to do is to take out the paper we have discussed on THE FEATURES OF A LITERARY EPIC. Carefully review the sheet, and then write a corresponding list of how *Beowulf* fits the criteria of a literary epic.

After you have jotted down examples from your memory of the reading, re-visit the text to find quotations from the text to support your contentions.

DRAFTING
Decide on a plan of attack for this writing assignment. Do you want to organize your paper thematically or chronologically? Once you have decided on your approach, you can compose your rough draft.

PROMPT
When you finish the rough draft of your composition, ask a student who sits near you to read it. After reading your rough draft, he/she should tell you what he/she liked best about your work, which parts were difficult to understand, and ways in which your work could be improved. Reread your paper considering your critic's comments, and make the corrections you think are necessary. Ask your classmate what he/she thought of each of the characters/events you chose for your assignment.

PROOFREADING
Do a final proofreading of your paper double-checking your grammar, spelling, organization, and the clarity of your ideas.

WRITING EVALUATION FORM - *Beowulf*

Name _____   Date _____

Grade _____

Circle One For Each Item:

Grammar: correct errors noted on paper

Spelling: correct errors noted on paper

Punctuation: correct errors noted on paper

Legibility: excellent   good   fair   poor

_____   excellent   good   fair   poor

_____   excellent   good   fair   poor

Strengths:

Weaknesses:

LESSON FIVE

Objectives
1. To assess student comprehension through a quiz on the Prologue through Chapter 13 of *Beowulf*
2. To give students experience researching nonfiction topics on *Beowulf*
3. To preview the study questions for Chapters 14-25
4. To familiarize students with the vocabulary from Chapters 14-25

Activity #1
Quiz - Distribute quizzes and give students about 10 minutes to complete them. (Note: The quizzes may either be the short answer study guides or the multiple choice version). Have students exchange papers. Grade the quizzes as a class. Collect the papers for recording the grades. (If you used the multiple choice version as a quiz, take a few minutes to discuss the answers for the short answer version if your students are using the short answer version for their study guides.)

Activity #2
Take students to the library/media center to find articles, books, etc. about nonfiction topics related to *Beowulf*. They should do their research on their own, although they can share their findings for the purpose of combined class reports as assigned by the teacher. Some suggested topics are:

Pagan influences in *Beowulf*
Beowulf as a Christian epic
Christian allegory in *Beowulf*
Did Beowulf really exist?
Did Hrothgar really exist?
Mythic influence in *Beowulf*
The relationship between the pagan and the Christian elements in *Beowulf*
Who were the monks that first transcribed *Beowulf*
The discoveries at Sutton Hoo

Activity #3
Give the students the remaining class time to preview the study questions and the vocabulary for Chapters 14-25.

NONFICTION ASSIGNMENT SHEET
(To be completed after reading the required nonfiction article)

Name _____ Date _____

Title of Nonfiction Read _____

Written By _____ Publication Date _____

I. Factual Summary: Write a short summary of the piece you read.

II. Vocabulary
    1. With which vocabulary words in the piece did you encounter some degree of difficulty?

    2. How did you resolve your lack of understanding with these words?

III. Interpretation: What was the main point the author wanted you to get from reading his work?

IV. Criticism
    1. With which points of the piece did you agree or find easy to accept? Why?

    2. With which points of the piece did you disagree or find difficult to believe? Why?

V. Personal Response: What do you think about this piece? OR How does this piece influence your ideas?

LESSON SIX

Objectives
1. To give the students time to complete their non-fiction research assignment in the library
2. To broaden the student's knowledge of the Anglo-Saxon Period through group work in the library

Activity #1
Students should take approximately half the period completing their non-fiction research on elements of the epic, *Beowulf*.

Activity #2
During the second half of the period, students should pair up with a partner to plan a class report on their findings.

LESSON SEVEN

Objectives
1. To review the study questions from Chapters 14-25 of *Beowulf*
2. To preview the study questions for Chapters 26-35 of *Beowulf*
3. To familiarize students with the vocabulary from Chapters 26-35 of *Beowulf*

Activity #1
Discuss the answers to the study questions from Chapters 14-25 of *Beowulf*. Ideally, it would be advantageous for pairs of students who have been pre-assigned these chapters to lead the discussion. The teacher should guide the discussion, when appropriate and fill in any gaps left by the students.

Activity #2
Give students the remaining class time to preview the study questions and the vocabulary for Chapters 26-35 of *Beowulf*.

NOTE: Time permitting-students should polish paired reports to be presented tomorrow

LESSON EIGHT

Objectives
1. To assess student comprehension through a quiz on Chapters 14-25
2. To widen the breadth of students' knowledge about the topics discussed or touched upon in *Beowulf*
3. To check students' nonfiction reading assignments

Activity #1
Quiz - Distribute quizzes and give students about 10 minutes to complete them. (Note: The quizzes may either be the short answer study guides or the multiple choice version). Have students exchange papers. Grade the quizzes as a class. Collect the papers for recording the grades. (If you used the multiple choice version as a quiz, take a few minutes to discuss the answers for the short answer version if your students are using the short answer version for their study guides.)

Activity #2
Ask each student to give a brief oral report about the nonfiction articles he/she read for the unit project assignment. Your criteria for evaluating this report will vary depending on the level of your students. You may wish for students to give a complete report without using notes of any kind, or you may want students to read directly from a written report, or you may want to do something in between these two extremes. Just make students aware of your criteria in ample time for them to prepare their reports.

Start with one student's report. After that, ask if anyone else in the class has read on a topic related to the first student's report. If no one has, choose another student at random. After each report, be sure to ask if anyone has a report related to the one just completed. That will help keep continuity during the discussion of the reports. After all reports on a topic are given, take a minute to hold a short class discussion about the information students have just heard.

LESSON NINE

Objective
    To read Chapters 26-35 of *Beowulf*

Activity #1
    Students should take this class time to read Chapters 26-35 of *Beowulf*. This assignment should be complete prior to the next class meeting.

LESSON TEN

Objectives
    1. To assess student comprehension through a quiz on Chapters 26-35 of *Beowulf*
    2. To evaluate students' oral reading from Chapters 36-43 of *Beowulf*

Activity #1
    Quiz - Distribute the multiple choice study guide quizzes for Chapters 26-35 and give students about 10 minutes to complete them.
    Have students exchange papers. Grade the quizzes as a class. Collect the papers for recording the grades.

Activity #2
    Give students time to preview the study questions and do the vocabulary worksheet for Chapters 36-43. When they have had ample time to complete this assignment, discuss the answers for the vocabulary worksheet.

Activity #3
    Have students begin reading Chapters 36-43 of *Beowulf* out loud in class. You probably know the best way to get readers within your class; pick students at random, ask for volunteers, or use whatever method works best for your group. If you have not yet completed an oral reading evaluation for your students this marking period, this would be a good opportunity to do so. A form is included with this unit for your convenience.

ORAL READING EVALUATION *Beowulf*

Name _____ Class ____ Date _____

SKILL	EXCELLENT	GOOD	AVERAGE	FAIR	POOR
Fluency	5	4	3	2	1
Clarity	5	4	3	2	1
Audibility	5	4	3	2	1
Pronunciation	5	4	3	2	1
_____	5	4	3	2	1
_____	5	4	3	2	1

Total ____   Grade ____

Comments:

LESSONS ELEVEN AND TWELVE

Objectives
1. To give students practice reading orally
2. To complete the oral reading evaluation from Chapters 36-43 of *Beowulf*
3. To give students the opportunity to practice writing persuasively

Activity #1

Have students continue reading Chapters 36-43 of *Beowulf* out loud in class. You probably know the best way to get readers within your class; pick students at random, ask for volunteers, or use whatever method works best for your group. If you have not yet completed an oral reading evaluation for your students this marking period, this would be a good opportunity to do so. A form is included with this unit for your convenience.

Activity #2

Distribute Writing Assignment #2 and discuss the directions in detail. Allow the remaining class time for students to complete the assignment. If they do not complete the assignment in the time remaining, it should be turned in on the following class day.

Follow-Up: After you have graded the assignments, have a writing conference with the students. After the writing conference, allow students to revise their papers using your suggestions and corrections. Give them about three days from the date they receive their papers to complete the revision. I suggest grading the revisions on an A-C-E scale (all revisions well-done, some revisions made, few or no revisions made). This will speed your grading time and still give some credit for the students' efforts.

WRITING ASSIGNMENT #2 - *Beowulf*

PROMPT

It has been written that Grendel's mother is, in fact, a sympathetic character in that she acts aggressively out of the love of her slain son. Despite the fact that she commits some bloody atrocities and takes on our hero, Beowulf, consider ways in which she may be seen as a victim reacting to unfortunate circumstances.

Your assignment is to write a journal entry from the perspective of Grendel's mother. Look at the situation from where and how she lives. Justify her actions by persuading us of her righteousness.

PREWRITING

A good place to start is to consider how Grendel's mother came to dwell in the lake of boiling blood in the first place. What role does fate play in how she lives out her days? What examples of affection do we see in Grendel's mother towards her monster-son?

Formulate an approach you want to take to the journal—and a time reference. Do you wish to compose the journal before the carnage at Hero begins? After Grendel's death? Remember to be sympathetic. Pay careful attention to the tone of your journal.

DRAFTING

You should begin your persuasive journal assignment by dating the entry and placing it in a "field of time" (*e.g. before Grendel's twelve-year assault on Herot, before Grendel's mother's revenge for the death of her son, Grendel's mother's anticipation of her struggle with Beowulf, etc.*)

As you begin to compose the draft, remember what you have learned about the reasons that Grendel's mother was forced to live where she did. Be sure to use some of these details as you compose a largely stream-of-consciousness piece.

To add interest to your composition, consider creating a unique "stationery" that Grendel's mother would use.

PROMPT

When you finish the rough draft of your paper, ask a student who sits near you to read it. After reading your rough draft, he/she should tell you what he/she liked best about your work, which parts were difficult to understand, and ways in which your work could be improved. Reread your paper considering your critic's comments, and make the corrections you think are necessary.

PROOFREADING

Do a final proofreading of your paper double-checking your grammar, spelling, organization, and the clarity of your ideas

WRITING EVALUATION FORM - *Beowulf*

Name _____   Date _____

Grade _____

Circle One For Each Item:

Grammar: correct errors noted on paper

Spelling: correct errors noted on paper

Punctuation: correct errors noted on paper

Legibility: excellent   good   fair   poor

_____   excellent   good   fair   poor

_____   excellent   good   fair   poor

LESSONS THIRTEEN AND FOURTEEN

Objectives
1. To review the main events and ideas from Chapters 36-43
2. To discuss the epic on a deeper than direct recall level
3. To focus on interpretation, critical analysis, and personal response

Activity #1
Discuss the answers to the study questions for Chapters 36-43.

Activity #2
Assign one of the Extra Discussion Questions/Writing Assignments to each of your students. Give students about fifteen minutes to formulate responses to their questions.* (Time needed with vary, depending on the level of your students.)

Activity #3
Discuss the students' responses to each of the Extra Discussion Questions you have selected. Be sure to guide the discussion so that no important points are left out. You may wish to jot down notes for students to copy (or have a sheet of notes already prepared for students to use for study purposes so they will pay attention and participate in the discussion without just copying from the board).

*Choose the questions from the Extra Discussion Questions/Writing Assignments which seem most appropriate for your students. A class discussion of these questions is most effective if students have been given the opportunity to formulate answers to the questions prior to the discussion. To this end, you may either have all the students formulate answers to all the questions, divide your class into groups and assign one or more questions to each group, or you could assign one question to each student in your class. The option you choose will make a difference in the amount of class time needed for this activity.

NOTE: The use of graphic organizers may be helpful to students in preparing their answers. Encourage them to use any diagrams or graphics that they feel are necessary.

NOTE: This activity will take two class periods.

EXTRA WRITING ASSIGNMENTS/DISCUSSION QUESTIONS - *Beowulf*

Interpretation
1. Who is the narrator of the *Beowulf* epic, and why is this important?

2. In what ways was Beowulf a model for Anglo-Saxon honor? What does he value?

3. What is foreshadowing? How is this used in Beowulf in his three battles as it relates to the armor he dons for each?

4. Why do the Danes and Hrothgar trust Beowulf so readily? What is their history together prior to the Grendel episode?

5. Why does Beowulf make the journey to help the Danes? How does this speak to Anglo-Saxon values?

6. Describe the relationship between Beowulf and Unferth.

7. Describe the relationship between Beowulf and Brecca.

8. What is the connection between Beowulf and Siegmund?

9. How does Beowulf's approach to fighting the dragon change from his attitude towards his battles with Grendel and his mother.

10. Why does Beowulf wish to see the treasure at the end of the epic?

Critical
11. Could Beowulf have avoided his destiny, according to the beliefs of the Anglo-Saxons? Explain.

12. Compare and contrast Beowulf's battle with Grendel and with Grendel's mother.

13. Discuss the significance of Grendel and his mother being called "the descendents of Cain."

14. How might the Christian monks have altered the original intent of the original *Beowulf* epic?

15. Discuss the significance of the lake of boiling blood that Beowulf must swim through to get to the cave of Grendel's mother.

16. Why is it significant that the end of Beowulf's life was caused by the actions of a slave.

17. Discuss any significance to Beowulf losing his power as he adorns more armor.

18. In what way is the Beowulf a distinctly "aristocratic poem", as it is called by the translator, Burton Raffel?

Beowulf Extra Discussion Questions Page 2

<u>Critical/Personal Response</u>

19. What elements of the *Beowulf* epic are believable?

20. What are the qualities of this poem that bring readers to it—even in the modern day?

21. If you were a Geat soldier hearing of the dragon, would you come to Beowulf's aid?

22. What qualities of friendship does Wiglaf show to Beowulf?

23. Define "fame" in your terms.

24. If "fate" had the dragon in the works for Beowulf, do you believe that there is a "fate" at work for everyman?

25. Are there any causes in the world worth fighting for in your opinion?

QUOTATIONS - *Beowulf*

1. And he (Hrothgar) thought of greatness and
   Resolved
   To build a hall that would hold his mighty
   Band and reach higher toward Haven than anything
   That had ever been known to the sons of men

2. A powerful monster, living down
   In the darkness, growled in pain, impatient
   As day after day the music rang…

3. So Hrothgar's men lived happy in his hall
   Till the monster stirred, that demon, that fiend,
   Grendel, who haunted the moors…

4. The Monster's
   Thoughts were as quick as his greed or his claws:

5. So Grendel ruled, fought with the righteous,
   One against many, and won; so Herot
   Stood empty, and stayed deserted for years,
   Twelve winters of grief for Hrothgar…

6. And sometimes they sacrificed to the old stone gods,
   Made heathen vows, hoping for Hell's
   Support…

7. Tell me your name,
   And your father's; no spies go further onto Danish
   Soil than you've come already.

8. This one favor you should not refuse me—
   That I alone and with the help of my men,
   May purge all evil from this hall.

9. You're Beowulf are you—the same
   Boastful fool who fought a swimming
   Match with Brecca…

10. It was said that God
    Himself had set a sentinel in Herot,
    Brought Beowulf as a guard against Grendel and a
    Shield
    Behind whom the king could safely rest.

11. He journeyed, forever joyless;
    Straight to the door, then snapped it open,
    Tore its iron fasteners with a touch
    And rushed angrily over the threshold.

12. But fate, that night, intended Grendel
    To gnaw the broken bones
    Of his last human supper.

13. No Dane doubted the victory, for the proof hanging high
    From the rafters where Beowulf had hung it, was
    The Monster's
    Arm, claw, shoulder and all.

14. Let me take you to my heart, make you my son too,
    And love you; preserve this passionate peace.

15. In her heart, that female horror, Grendel's
    Mother, living in the murky cold lake
    Assigned her since Cain had killed his only
    Brother, slain his father's son
    With an angry sword.

16. Each of us will come to the end of this life
    On Earth; he who can earn it should fight
    For the glory of his name; fame after death
    Is the noblest of goals.

17. Hrunting could not hurt her.

18. The monster's hall was full of
    Rich treasures, but all that Beowulf took
    Was Grendel's head and the hilt of the giants'
    Jeweled sword…

19. Be not
    As Hermod once was to my people, too proud
    To care what their hearts hid…

20. Beloved Beowulf, best of warriors,
    Choose instead eternal happiness;
    Push away pride!

21. You've turned Danes
    And Geats into brothers…

22. He was old
   With years and wisdom, fifty winters
   A king, when a dragon awoke from its darkness
   And dreams and brought terror to his people.

23. But the thief had not come to steal; he stole
   And roused the dragon, not from desire
   But need.

24. But Beowulf's heart was heavy:
   His soul sensed how close fate
   Had come, felt something, not fear but knowledge
   Of old age.

25. And only one of them remained,
   Stood there, miserable, remembering,
   As a good man must, what kinship should mean.

26. He took us for soldiers, for men.

27. I'd rather burn myself than see
   Flames swirling around my lord.

28. But fate had decreed that the Geats' great king
   Would be no better for any weapon.

29. My days have gone by as fate willed, waiting
   For its word to be spoken, ruling as well
   As I knew how, swearing no unholy oaths,
   Seeking no lying wars.

30. War came and you ran like cowards, dropped
   Your swords as soon as the danger was real.

31. Twelve of the bravest Geats
   Rode their horses around the tower,
   Telling their sorrow, telling stories
   Of their dead king and his greatness, his glory,
   Praising him for heroic deeds, for a life
   As noble as his name."

LESSON FIFTEEN

<u>Objective</u>
　　　To review all of the vocabulary work done in this unit

<u>Activity</u>
　　　Choose one (or more) of the vocabulary review activities listed below and spend your class period as directed in the activity. Some of the materials for these review activities are located in the Vocabulary Resource Materials section in this LitPlan.

VOCABULARY REVIEW ACTIVITIES

1. Divide your class into two teams and have an old-fashioned spelling or definition bee.

2. Give each of your students (or students in groups of two, three or four) an *Beowulf* Vocabulary Word Search Puzzle. The person (group) to find all of the vocabulary words in the puzzle first wins.

3. Give students an *Beowulf* Vocabulary Word Search Puzzle without the word list. The person or group to find the most vocabulary words in the puzzle wins.

4. Use an *Beowulf* Vocabulary Crossword Puzzle. Put the puzzle onto a transparency on the overhead projector (so everyone can see it), and do the puzzle together as a class.

5. Give students an *Beowulf* Vocabulary Matching Worksheet to do.

6. Divide your class into two teams. Use *Beowulf* vocabulary words with their letters jumbled as a word list. Student 1 from Team A faces off against Student 1 from Team B. You write the first jumbled word on the board. The first student (1A or 1B) to unscramble the word wins the chance for his/her team to score points. If 1A wins the jumble, go to student 2A and give him/her a definition. He/she must give you the correct spelling of the vocabulary word which fits that definition. If he/she does, Team A scores a point, and you give student 3A a definition for which you expect a correctly spelled matching vocabulary word. Continue giving Team A definitions until some team member makes an incorrect response. An incorrect response sends the game back to the jumbled-word face off, this time with students 2A and 2B. Instead of repeating giving definitions to the first few students of each team, continue with the student after the one who gave the last incorrect response on the team. For example, if Team B wins the jumbled-word face-off, and student 5B gave the last incorrect answer for Team B, you would start this round of definition questions with student 6B, and so on. The team with the most points wins!

7. Have students write a story in which they correctly use as many vocabulary words as possible. Have students read their compositions orally! Post the most original compositions on your bulletin board.

LESSON SIXTEEN

Objectives
1. To give students the opportunity to express their personal ideas
2. To give students the opportunity to think about their own mortality and their legacy to future generations
3. To give the teacher the opportunity to evaluate students' writing

Activity

Distribute Writing Assignment #3. Discuss the directions in detail and give students the remainder of the class period to complete this assignment. Collect the papers at the end of the class period.

Follow-Up:

After you have graded the assignments, have a writing conference with the students. After the writing conference, allow students to revise their papers using your suggestions and corrections. Give them about three days from the date they receive their papers to complete the revision. I suggest grading the revisions on an A-C-E scale (all revisions well-done, some revisions made, few or no revisions made). This will speed your grading time and still give some credit for the students' efforts.

WRITING ASSIGNMENT #3 - *Beowulf*

PROMPT

Everyone hopes that after their death they will not be forgotten. We hope to live our lives in such a fashion that our deeds and/or our words will outlive us. Beowulf was very much aware of the transitory nature of life, and he made it his mission to be famous so that his name would not be extinguished upon his death.

Oftentimes luck and longevity play important roles in how we are perceived after death, but more importantly, it is how we live our lives that will determine our fame and "immortality". You can increase your chances of being remembered by taking active measures during your life to insure your fame.

Your assignment is to think of a way that you can combine one of your passions or desires with a plan to become famous after your death. Make a detailed plan for the execution of this plan and use your imagination!

PREWRITING

A good way to start is to focus on your passions. What do you love to do? What ideas do you possess that could possible succeed you? Jot these possibilities down on a piece of paper. Make detailed notes of how you could achieve immortality.

Now, stop and think about what you can practically do to achieve these aspirations. Make a list. Are there certain steps that you must follow first? Is there anything prohibiting you from advancing towards these dreams at this point in your life?

DRAFTING

You should begin with an opening paragraph in which you grab the attention of the reader by announcing your lofty ambition. Be precise about your reasons for this desire in the first paragraph.

The body of your composition should provide a plan of action or a timeline of what you must accomplish in your life to insure fame after your death. Be certain that each supporting paragraph is well-developed.

Write a concluding paragraph about the likelihood of your success given the plan that you have outlined in your paper.

PROOFREADING

Do a final proofreading of your paper double-checking your grammar, spelling, organization, and the clarity of your ideas.

WRITING EVALUATION FORM - *Beowulf*

Name _____   Date _____

Grade _____

Circle One For Each Item:

Grammar:	correct errors noted on paper
Spelling:	correct errors noted on paper
Punctuation:	correct errors noted on paper
Legibility:	excellent good fair poor
_____	excellent good fair poor
_____	excellent good fair poor

Strengths:

Weaknesses:

Comments/Suggestions:

LESSON SEVENTEEN

Objective
　　To review the main ideas and events in *Beowulf*

Activity #1
　　Choose one of the review games/activities suggested in this unit and spend your class time as outlined there. Some materials for these activities are located in the extra activities section of this unit.

Activity #2
　　Remind students that the Unit Test will be in the next class meeting. Stress the review of the study guides and their class notes as a last minute, brush-up review for homework.

REVIEW GAMES/ACTIVITIES *Beowulf*

1. Ask the class to make up a unit test for *Beowulf*. The test should have 4 sections: matching, true/false, short answer, and essay. Students may use 1/2 period to make the test and then swap papers and use the other 1/2 class period to take a test a classmate has devised. (open book) You may want to use the unit test included in this packet or take questions from the students' unit tests to formulate your own test.

2. Take 1/2 period for students to make up true and false questions (including the answers). Collect the papers and divide the class into two teams. Draw a big tic-tac-toe board on the chalk board. Make one team X and one team O. Ask questions to each side, giving each student one turn. If the question is answered correctly, that students' team's letter (X or O) is placed in the box. If the answer is incorrect, no letter is placed in the box. The object is to get three in a row like tic-tac-toe. You may want to keep track of the number of games won for each team.

3. Take 1/2 period for students to make up questions (true/false and short answer). Collect the questions. Divide the class into two teams. You'll alternate asking questions to individual members of teams A & B (like in a spelling bee). The question keeps going from A to B until it is correctly answered, then a new question is asked. A correct answer does not allow the team to get another question. Correct answers are +2 points; incorrect answers are -1 point.

4. Have students pair up and quiz each other from their study guides and class notes.

5. Give students an *Beowulf* crossword puzzle to complete.

6. Divide your class into two teams. Use *Beowulf* crossword words with their letters jumbled as a word list. Student 1 from Team A faces off against Student 1 from Team B. You write the first jumbled word on the board. The first student (1A or 1B) to unscramble the word wins the chance for his/her team to score points. If 1A wins the jumble, go to student 2A and give him/her a clue. He/she must give you the correct word which matches that clue. If he/she does, Team A scores a point, and you give student 3A a clue for which you expect another correct response. Continue giving Team A clues until some team member makes an incorrect response. An incorrect response sends the game back to the jumbled-word face off, this time with students 2A and 2B. Instead of repeating giving clues to the first few students of each team, continue with the student after the one who gave the last incorrect response on the team. For example, if Team B wins the jumbled-word face-off, and student 5B gave the last incorrect answer for Team B, you would start this round of clue questions with student 6B, and so on. The team with the most points wins!

Review Games Page 2

8. Play What's My Line?. This is similar to the old television show. Students assume the roles of different characters from the epic. One student gives clues to the class, or to a panel of contestants. The contestants try to guess the identity of the guest. Students may enjoy assisting you in creating rules and procedures for the game.

9. Play Jeopardy. Divide the class into two groups. Assign each group a category or book from the epic and have them devise answers for that category. Play the game according to the television show procedures.

10. Play Drawing in the Details. This is similar to Pictionary. Divide students into teams. A student from one team draws a scene from the epic. (You may want to specify the Book or section.) Drawings should be kept simple, to keep the pace lively. Students in the opposing team locate the scene in their books and read it aloud. If they are incorrect, the illustrator's team has a chance to guess. Involve students in setting up a scoring system and any other necessary rules.

LESSON EIGHTEEN

Objective
   To test the students understanding of the main ideas and themes in *Beowulf*

Activity #1
   Distribute the unit tests. Go over the instructions in detail and allow the students the entire class period to complete the exam.

NOTES ABOUT THE UNIT TESTS IN THIS UNIT:
   There are 5 different unit tests which follow.
   There are two short answer tests which are based primarily on facts from the epic. The answer key for short answer unit test 1 follows the student test. The answer key for short answer test 2 follows the student short answer unit test 2.
   There is one advanced short answer unit test. It is based on the extra discussion questions and quotations. Use the matching key for short answer unit test 2 to check the matching section of the advanced short answer unit test. There is no key for the short answer questions and quotations. The answers will be based on the discussions you have had during class.
   There are two multiple choice unit tests. Following the two unit tests, you will find an answer sheet on which students should mark their answers. The same answer sheet should be used for both tests; however, students' answers will be different for each test. Following the students' answer sheet for the multiple choice tests you will find your two keys: one for multiple choice test 1 and one for multiple choice test 2. If you follow the directions at the top of each of those pages, you should be able to overlay your answer key on the students' answer sheets and easily grade the papers.
   The short answer tests have a vocabulary section. You should choose 10 of the vocabulary words from this unit, read them orally and have the students write them down. Then, either have students write a definition or use the words in sentences.

   Use these words for the vocabulary section of the advanced short answer unit test:

   ascribed   heathen   solace
   ruminative   furrows   niggardly
   reparation   hilt   malice
   writhing   pyre   venom

Activity #2
   Collect all test papers and assigned books prior to the end of the class period.

UNIT TESTS

SHORT ANSWER UNIT TEST 1 - *Beowulf*

I. Matching/Identify

____ 1. Beowulf   A. Son of Hrothgar and Welthow

____ 2. Hrothgar   B. Beowulf's ancestral sword

____ 3. Welthow   C. Beowulf's second foe

____ 4. Unferth   D. King of the Geats

____ 5. Brecca   E. Hrothgar's friend; killed by Grendel's mother

____ 6. Siegmund   F. King of the Danes

____ 7. Higlac   G. Prince of the Geats, our hero

____ 8. Higd   H. Unferth's sword

____ 9. Grendel   I. Higlac's successor

____ 10. Grendel's mother J. Hrothgar's mead hall

____ 11. dragon   K. He kills Beowulf

____ 12. Herot   L. Past warrior who also killed a dragon

____ 13. Edgetho   M. Hrothgar's "gold-ringed" queen

____ 14. Esher   N. Higlac's wife

____ 15. Wulfgar   O. Helps Beowulf slay the dragon

____ 16. Herdred   P. Beowulf's first nemesis

____ 17. Hrethric   Q. Swedish prince; introduces Beowulf to Hrothgar

____ 18. Hrunting   R. Braggart who questioned Beowulf's bravery

____ 19. Wiglaf   S. Beowulf's father

____ 20. Nagling   T. Beowulf beats him in swimming match

Beowulf Short Answer Unit Test 1 Page 2

II. Short Answer

1. What were the basic virtues prized by Anglo-Saxon society?

2. Why doesn't Grendel attack Hrothgar?

3. Identify: Unferth. Why does he seem to be perplexed by Beowulf's stories?

4. How does Grendel respond when he comes to Herot? Describe his reaction to seeing the sleeping Geats.

5. Who is Siegmund? Why is his story recounted?

6. How were the bodies of the dead disposed of in Anglo-Saxon times?

7. According to Beowulf, what is the only thing that survives death?

8. How does Beowulf eventually slay Grendel's mother?

9. What does Beowulf think has brought on the wrath of the dragon?

10. What role does fate play in Beowulf's demise, according to Wiglaf?

Beowulf Short Answer Unit Test 1 Page 3

III. Quotations: Explain the importance or significance of each of the following quotations:

1. A powerful monster, living down
   In the darkness, growled in pain, impatient
   As day after day the music rang…

2. He journeyed, forever joyless;
   Straight to the door, then snapped it open,
   Tore its iron fasteners with a touch
   And rushed angrily over the threshold.

3. Hrunting could not hurt her.

4. But Beowulf's heart was heavy:
   His soul sensed how close fate
   Had come, felt something, not fear but knowledge
   Of old age.

5. He took us for soldiers, for men.

6. Twelve of the bravest Geats
   Rode their horses around the tower.
   Telling their sorrow, telling stories
   Of their dead king and his greatness, his glory,
   Praising him for heroic deeds, for a life
   As noble as his name.

Beowulf Short Answer Unit Test 1 Page 4

III. Essay

    Discuss the notion of the "dragon" as a metaphor for the fate that the Anglo-Saxons believed was was in store for everyman. Why is the dragon the cause of Beowulf's undoing? Why not a stronger foe?

Beowulf Short Answer Unit Test 1 Page 5

IV. Vocabulary

Write down the vocabulary words. Go back later and write down the correct definition for each word.

1.

2.

3.

4.

5.

6.

7.

8.

9.

10.

SHORT ANSWER UNIT TEST 1 ANSWER KEY – *Beowulf*

I. Matching/Identify

1.	G	11.	K
2.	F	12.	J
3.	M	13.	S
4.	R	14.	E
5.	T	15.	Q
6.	L	16.	I
7.	D	17.	A
8.	N	18.	H
9.	P	19.	O
10.	C	20.	B

II. Short Answer

1. What were the basic virtues prized by Anglo-Saxon society?
    Strength, courage, bravery, and generosity were the virtues prized by the Anglo-Saxons.

2. Why doesn't Grendel attack Hrothgar?
    Grendel does not dare touch Hrothgar as he is protected by God.

3. Identify: Unferth. Why does he seem to be perplexed by Beowulf's stories?
    Unferth is a Danish nobleman who is angry that any warrior anywhere has achieved greater glory than he has. Unferth calls Beowulf a "boastful fool".

4. How does Grendel respond when he comes to Herot? Describe his reaction to seeing the sleeping Geats.
    Grendel tears the hinges off the door at Herot and is thrilled at the sight of the sleeping Geats—expecting to fill his belly with their meat.

5. Who is Siegmund? Why is his story recounted?
    Siegmund was a legendary hero to the Danes. Tales of his exploits were passed down through generations. Beowulf's victory over Grendel was likened to Siegmund's great feats.

6. How were the bodies of the dead disposed of in Anglo-Saxon times?
   In Anglo-Saxon times, the bodies of dead soldiers were burned on a funeral pyre.

7. According to Beowulf, what is the only thing that survives death?
   The only thing that survives death, according to Beowulf, is glory and fame.

8. How does Beowulf eventually slay Grendel's mother?
   Beowulf discovers a sword hanging on the wall of the cave and slices her neck through.

9. What does Beowulf think has brought on the wrath of the dragon?
   Beowulf felt that because he as a king had broken God's law, the dragon wreaked his wrath upon the Geats.

10. What role does fate play in Beowulf's demise, according to Wiglaf?
    Wiglaf tells the people that fate had the dragon in store for Beowulf. It was "meant to be".

III. Quotations: Explain the importance or significance of each of the following quotations:

ANSWERS WILL VARY DEPENDING ON YOUR CLASS DISCUSSIONS AND THE LEVEL OF YOUR CLASS.

IV. Essay

Discuss the notion of the "dragon" as a metaphor for the fate that the Anglo-Saxons believed was in store for everyman. Why is the dragon the cause of Beowulf's undoing? Why not a stronger foe?

ANSWERS WILL VARY DEPENDING ON YOUR CLASS DISCUSSIONS AND THE LEVEL OF YOUR CLASS.

V. Vocabulary
   Choose 10 of the vocabulary words. Read them orally for students to write down.

SHORT ANSWER UNIT TEST 2 - *Beowulf*

I. Matching/Identify

____ 1. Beowulf		A.	Beowulf beats him in a swimming match
____ 2. Hrothgar		B.	Beowulf's second foe
____ 3. Welthow		C.	Beowulf's ancestral sword
____ 4. Unferth		D.	King of the Danes
____ 5. Brecca		E.	Hrothgar's friend; killed by Grendel's mother
____ 6. Siegmund		F.	King of the Geats
____ 7. Higlac		G.	Prince of the Geats, our hero
____ 8. Higd		H.	Braggart who questioned Beowulf's bravery
____ 9. Grendel		I.	Helps Beowulf slay the dragon
____ 10. Grendel's mother		J.	Hrothgar's "gold-ringed" queen
____ 11. dragon		K.	Beowulf's father
____ 12. Herot		L.	Past warrior who also killed a dragon
____ 13. Edgetho		M.	Hrothgar's mead hall
____ 14. Esher		N.	Beowulf's first nemesis
____ 15. Wulfgar		O.	Higlac's successor
____ 16. Herdred		P.	Higlac's wife
____ 17. Hrethric		Q.	Swedish prince; introduces Beowulf to Hrothgar
____ 18. Hrunting		R.	Unferth's sword
____ 19. Wiglaf		S.	He kills Beowulf
____ 20. Nagling		T.	Son of Hrothgar and Welthow

Beowulf Unit Short Answer Test 2 Page 2
Short Answer

1. Why does the editor refer to the *Beowulf* epic as "essentially an aristocratic poem"?

2. What is Grendel's lineage? Why is he described as being "born of Cain"?

3. What one request does Beowulf make of Hrothgar?

4. Describe Welthow.

5. What happens when Grendel reaches for Beowulf?

6. What is Grendel's mother's motive in coming to Herot?

7. What is the significance of the word, Hrunting?

8. What does Beowulf take with him as souvenirs of his victory over Grendel's mother?

9. What large event happens fifty years into Beowulf's reign?

10. What do Beowulf's men do as he is taking on the dragon?

Beowulf Unit Short Answer Test 2 Page 3

III. Quotations
   Explain the significance of the following quotations:

1. The Monster's
   Thoughts were as quick as his claws.

2. But fate, that night, intended Grendel
   To gnaw the broken bones
   Of his last human supper.

3. Beloved Beowulf, best of warriors,
   Choose instead eternal happiness;
   Push away pride!

4. You've turned Danes
   And Geats into brothers.

5. But the thief had not come to steal; he stole
   And roused the dragon, not from desire
   But need.

6. I'd rather burn myself than see
   Flames swirling around my lord.

Beowulf Short Answer Unit Test 2 Page 4

IV. Essay

    Discuss why with each quest and challenge that Beowulf encounters he dons more armor and weapons. How could this been seen as a metaphor for his waning strength and faith, according to the Christian translators of the text?

Beowulf Short Answer Unit Test 2 page 5

IV. Vocabulary

    Write down the vocabulary words. Go back later and write down the correct definitions for the words.

1.

2.

3.

4.

5.

6.

7.

8.

9.

10.

ANSWER KEY: SHORT ANSWER UNIT TEST 2 - *Beowulf*

I. Matching/Identify

1.	G	11.	S
2.	D	12.	M
3.	J	13.	K
4.	H	14.	E
5.	A	15.	Q
6.	L	16.	O
7.	F	17.	T
8.	P	18.	R
9.	N	19.	I
10.	B	20.	C

II. Short Answer

1. Why does the editor refer to the *Beowulf* epic as "essentially an aristocratic poem"?
   Beowulf is concerned mainly with the large issue of kings and kingship. The other classes of society are not represented.

2. What is Grendel's lineage? Why is he described as being "born of Cain"?
   Grendel is described as being spawned in slime by two of the monsters who were descendents of the Biblical character, Cain, who was banished from God for committing the murder of his brother.

3. What one request does Beowulf make of Hrothgar?
   Beowulf asks Hrothgar to allow him and his men alone to drive Grendel from Herot.

4. Describe Welthow.
   Welthow is Hrothgar's "gold-ringed Queen". She is described as a noble woman who "knows what is right."

5. What happens when Grendel reaches for Beowulf?
   Beowulf grabs Grendel and begins a hand to hand battle with him.

6. What is Grendel's mother's motive in coming to Herot?
   Grendel's mother comes to Herot seeking revenge for the loss of her son.

7. What is the significance of the word, Hrunting?
   Hrunting is the sword given to Beowulf by Unferth. It has a shining blade and was hardened in blood.

8. What does Beowulf take with him as souvenirs of his victory over Grendel's mother?
   As souvenirs of his victory, Beowulf takes Grendel's head and the hilt of his "magnificent sword."

9. What large event happens fifty years into Beowulf's reign?
   After fifty years on the throne, Beowulf is faced with an awakening dragon that has come to terrorize the Geats.

10. What do Beowulf's men do as he is taking on the dragon?
    Beowulf's followers ran for their lives as their leader took on the dragon.

III. Quotations: Explain the importance or significance of each of the following quotations:

ANSWERS WILL VARY DEPENDING ON YOUR CLASS DISCUSSIONS AND THE LEVEL OF YOUR CLASS.

IV. Essay

Discuss why with each quest and challenge that Beowulf encounters he dons more armor and weapons. How could this be seen as a metaphor for his waning strength, according to the Christian translators of the text?

ANSWERS WILL VARY DEPENDING ON YOUR CLASS DISCUSSIONS AND THE LEVEL OF YOUR CLASS.

V. Vocabulary
   Choose 10 of the vocabulary words. Read them orally for students to write down.

MULTIPLE CHOICE UNIT TEST 1 - *Beowulf*

I. Matching/Identify

____ 1. Beowulf	A.	Son of Hrothgar and Welthow
____ 2. Hrothgar	B.	Beowulf's ancestral sword
____ 3. Welthow	C.	Beowulf's second foe
____ 4. Unferth	D.	King of the Geats
____ 5. Brecca	E.	Hrothgar's friend; killed by Grendel's mother
____ 6. Siegmund	F.	King of the Danes
____ 7. Higlac	G.	Prince of the Geats, our hero
____ 8. Higd	H.	Unferth's sword
____ 9. Grendel	I.	Higlac's successor
____ 10. Grendel's mother	J.	Hrothgar's mead hall
____ 11. dragon	K.	He kills Beowulf
____ 12. Herot	L.	Past warrior who also killed a dragon
____ 13. Edgetho	M.	Hrothgar's "gold-ringed" queen
____ 14. Esher	N.	Higlac's wife
____ 15. Wulfgar	O.	Helps Beowulf slay the dragon
____ 16. Herdred	P.	Beowulf's first nemesis
____ 17. Hrethric	Q.	Swedish prince; introduces Beowulf to Hrothgar
____ 18. Hrunting	R.	Braggart who questioned Beowulf's bravery
____ 19. Wiglaf	S.	Beowulf's father
____ 20. Nagling	T.	Beowulf beats him in swimming match

Beowulf Multiple Choice Unit Test 1 Page 2

II. Multiple Choice

1. *Beowulf* is essentially-
    a. One of many surviving epics from the period
    b. An aristocratic poem about kings and kingship
    c. A poor representation of Anglo-Saxon life
    d. A poem about the working middle class Anglo-Saxons

2. The first writer of Beowulf was thought to have been-
    a. A Christian monk
    b. A court poet
    c. A member of Anglo-Saxon royalty
    d. A knight

3. What transpired in Herot to evoke the anger of Grendel?
    a. Grendel grew tired of the music and happiness at Herot.
    b. Hrothgar used Grendel's belongings in the construction of Herot.
    c. The Danes bragged that they were stronger than Grendel.
    d. Nothing; Grendel just was ready for a fight.

4. Why doesn't Grendel attack Hrothgar?
    a. Hrothgar wears a protective cloak.
    b. Hrothgar is physically stronger than the monster, and Grendel knows it.
    c. As part of a prior treaty, Grendel cannot attack Hrothgar.
    d. Hrothgar is protected by God himself.

5. Who is the warrior that Beowulf defeated in a swimming competition?
    a. Brecca
    b. Higlac
    c. Unferth
    d. Herdred

6. Characterize the battle between Grendel and Beowulf.
    a. Grendel has the upper hand.
    b. Beowulf loses his courage and retreats.
    c. Beowulf is successfully supported by over a dozen fierce Geat warriors.
    d. Beowulf battles Grendel alone and without weapons.

7. What happens at the end of Beowulf's battle against Grendel?
    a. Mortally wounded, Grendel returns to his cave to die.
    b. Grendel's body lies dead at Herot.
    c. Beowulf is mortally wounded by Grendel.
    d. Beowulf hangs Grendel's head from the rafters of Herot.

Beowulf Multiple Choice Unit Test 1 Page 3

8. What happened to the bodies of the dead soldiers during Anglo-Saxon times?
    a. They were buried with their armor on.
    b. They were sent to sea in an uncaptained ship.
    c. They were left on the field to become part of nature.
    d. They were burned on a funeral pyre.

9. Who does Grendel's mother kill when she enters Herot?
    a. Hrothgar
    b. Hrothgar's best friend, Esher
    c. The bragging Danish warrior, Unferth
    d. Beowulf's father, Edgetho

10. According to Beowulf, what is the only thing that survives death?
    a. Loyalty
    b. Writing
    c. Families
    d. Fame

11. How does Beowulf kill Grendel's mother?
    a. He finds a sword on the wall of the cave and slices her in two
    b. He kills her with Unferth's sword
    c. He destroys her with his bare hands
    d. He is helped by his men in killing Grendel's mother

12. To what does Beowulf attribute his victory over Grendel's mother?
    a. Beowulf attributes his victory to God's grace.
    b. Beowulf tells Hrothgar that his pride granted him victory over Grendel's mother.
    c. Beowulf believes he won because he was stronger than Grendel's mother.
    d. Beowulf credits his men for his victory over Grendel's mother.

13. What realization does Hrothgar make as Beowulf departs?
    a. Hrothgar realizes that Beowulf was very self-centered.
    b. Hrothgar acknowledges that Beowulf had a very large ego.
    c. Hrothgar discovers that Beowulf wasn't very honest with him.
    d. Hrothgar knows that he will never see Beowulf again.

14. How does Higlac reward Beowulf for his feats?
    a. Higlac sends Beowulf back to the Danes.
    b. Higlac imprisons Beowulf because he is threatened by his accomplishments.
    c. Higlac gives Beowulf his grandfather's sword and lots of property.
    d. Higlac gives Beowulf his daughter's hand in marriage.

Beowulf Multiple Choice Unit Test 1 Page 4

15. What did the slave steal from the dragon?
    a. His fire
    b. A jeweled cup
    c. 12 bags of gold
    d. Magic armor

16. Who first owned the treasure guarded by the dragon?
    a. The last survivor of a noble race
    b. Another dragon
    c. Higlac
    d. God

17. Why does Beowulf announce that he is going to fight the dragon alone?
    a. This is a trick; Beowulf wants the dragon to think he is going to fight him alone, but in fact he will have his warriors with him for support.
    b. Beowulf knows that he alone possesses the strength to defeat the dragon.
    c. Beowulf wants to keep all of the treasure for himself.
    d. Beowulf feels that it is his duty as a king to take on the dragon himself.

18. How does Beowulf feel about his upcoming battle against the dragon?
    a. Beowulf is confident that he can defeat the dragon.
    b. Beowulf sees it as all in a day's work for a warrior-king.
    c. Beowulf has a sense of doom just prior to the battle against the dragon.
    d. Beowulf is hopeful that he can win one more victory for the Geats.

19. What is Wiglaf's response to Beowulf's people after the death of Beowulf?
    a. He makes his peace with them.
    b. He admonishes them for their cowardice.
    c. He joins them in celebrating Beowulf's life.
    d. He accepts their gratitude graciously for helping to slay the dragon.

20. What is the role of the twelve horsemen?
    a. They become Wiglaf's administrative council.
    b. They travel to the Danes to tell them that Beowulf has been killed.
    c. They remain at Beowulf's tomb to tell the tale of his great fame and glory.
    d. They begin a war that plunges the Geats once more into turmoil.

Beowulf Multiple Choice Unit Test 1 Page 5

III. Composition

1. In what ways was Beowulf a model for Anglo-Saxon honor? What does he value?

2. What is the connection between Beowulf and Siegmund?

3. Compare and contrast Beowulf's battle with Grendel and with Grendel's mother.

4. Discuss the significance of the lake of boiling blood that Beowulf must swim through to get to the cave of Grendel's mother.

5. Why is it significant that the end of Beowulf's life was caused by the actions of a slave?

Beowulf Multiple Choice Unit Test 1 Page 6
IV. Vocabulary - Match the correct definitions to the words.

____ 1.	tripartite	A.	the handle of a sword or dagger
____ 2.	ruminative	B.	a group or accumulation
____ 3.	omens	C.	tight
____ 4.	taut	D.	miserable, pitiable
____ 5.	talons	E.	evil intent
____ 6.	hilt	F.	prophetic signs
____ 7.	runic	G.	burning
____ 8.	tarnish	H.	consisting of three parts
____ 9.	billowing	I.	a discoloration of metal
____ 10.	malice	J.	stones roughly placed together
____ 11.	hag	K.	meditative, pondering
____ 12.	wretched	L.	bursting with flame or smoke
____ 13.	earthen	M.	a repulsive old woman
____ 14.	unaided	N.	anxiety or concern
____ 15.	belching	O.	made of dirt
____ 16.	solace	P.	claws
____ 17.	charring	Q.	comfort in sorrow
____ 18.	hoards	R.	flowing, rising on the wind
____ 19.	cobbled	S.	unassisted
____ 20.	solicitude	T.	an ancient, interlacing script

MULTIPLE CHOICE UNIT TEST 2 - *Beowulf*

I. Matching/Identify

____ 1. Beowulf	A.	Beowulf beats him in a swimming match
____ 2. Hrothgar	B.	Beowulf's second foe
____ 3. Welthow	C.	Beowulf's ancestral sword
____ 4. Unferth	D.	King of the Danes
____ 5. Brecca	E.	Hrothgar's friend; killed by Grendel's mother
____ 6. Siegmund	F.	King of the Geats
____ 7. Higlac	G.	Prince of the Geats, our hero
____ 8. Higd	H.	Braggart who questioned Beowulf's bravery
____ 9. Grendel	I.	Helps Beowulf slay the dragon
____ 10. Grendel's mother	J.	Hrothgar's "gold-ringed" queen
____ 11. dragon	K.	Beowulf's father
____ 12. Herot	L.	Past warrior who also killed a dragon
____ 13. Edgetho	M.	Hrothgar's mead hall
____ 14. Esher	N.	Beowulf's first nemesis
____ 15. Wulfgar	O.	Higlac's successor
____ 16. Herdred	P.	Higlac's wife
____ 17. Hrethric	Q.	Swedish prince; introduces Beowulf to Hrothgar
____ 18. Hrunting	R.	Unferth's sword
____ 19. Wiglaf	S.	He kills Beowulf
____ 20. Nagling	T.	Son of Hrothgar and Welthow

Beowulf Multiple Choice Unit Test 2 Page 2

II. Multiple Choice

1. In its original form, *Beowulf* was-
    A. Short and lyrical
    B. Orally transmitted
    C. Written in French
    D. Composed by royalty

2. The most important people to the Anglo-Saxons were the-
    A. Priests
    B. Sorcerers
    C. Explorers
    D. Warriors

3. Why was Grendel exiled?
    A. He was disrespectful to Hrothgar.
    B. He broke the rules of Anglo-Saxon society.
    C. He was considered a descendent of Cain and exiled by God
    D. He elected to live away from humans.

4. What one request does Beowulf make of Hrothgar?
    A. He asks Hrothgar to accompany him on his search for Grendel.
    B. He asks Hrothgar to allow him and his men alone to drive Grendel from Herot.
    C. He asks to be made heir to the throne of Denmark.
    D. He asks Hrothgar for money for the quest.

5. Who is the Danish warrior who questions Beowulf's bravery in front of Hrothgar?
    A. Wulfgar
    B. Wiglaf
    C. Edgetho
    D. Unferth

6. How is Welthow described on several occasions?
    A. Gold-ringed
    B. Icy
    C. Jealous
    D. Intelligent

7. Beowulf's battle with Grendel is likened to this great Danish warrior-
    A. Hrothgar
    B. Higlac
    C. Siegmund
    D. Unferth

Beowulf Multiple Choice Unit Test 2 Page 3

8. What does Hrothgar proclaim after seeing the arm of Grendel hanging from Herot?
   A. That Beowulf shall succeed him as king.
   B. That Beowulf shall be considered as a son.
   C. That he will not be satisfied until he sees the remainder of the slain monster.
   D. That Beowulf should never return to his homeland.

9. How long had Grendel's mother lived in the subterranean lake?
   A. Grendel's mother lived under the lake since Grendel's death.
   B. Grendel's mother lived under the lake since Cain killed his brother Abel.
   C. Grendel's mother lived under the lake since she was sent there by Hrothgar.
   D. Grendel's mother lived under the lake since her cave on the surface was destroyed by Beowulf and his men.

10. Characterize the lake under which Grendel's mother lived.
    A. Bottomless and composed of hot, boiling blood
    B. Shallow, but treacherous
    C. Covered with sheets of jagged ice
    D. Calm with black water

11. What do Hrothgar's men find on their way to search for Grendel's mother?
    A. A stash of weapons
    B. Esher's head
    C. A horrible storm
    D. A vast treasure

12. What does Beowulf do when he finds Grendel's body?
    A. He throws it in the lake.
    B. He uses it as a shield against Grendel's mother.
    C. He chops off its head.
    D. He mocks it.

13. Before Beowulf leaves for home, what does Hrothgar caution him against?
    A. Pride
    B. Vanity
    C. Self-centeredness
    D. Deceit

14. For how long does Beowulf peacefully rule the Geats?
    A. 12 winters
    B. Until he dies
    C. 50 years
    D. One month

Beowulf Multiple Choice Unit Test 2 Page 4

15. What did the slave steal from the dragon?
    A. His fire
    B. A jeweled cup
    C. 12 bags of gold
    D. Magic armor

16. What does Beowulf think has brought on the wrath of the dragon?
    A. Beowulf feels that the greed of the Geats has awakened the wrath of the dragon.
    B. Beowulf feels that the slave is to blame.
    C. Beowulf blames his own lack of piety for angering the dragon.
    D. Beowulf thinks fate has brought out the dragon's wrath.

17. What do Beowulf's men do when he goes to fight the dragon?
    A. They run and hide.
    B. They rally behind him.
    C. They travel to seek the help of the Danes.
    D. They are not aware that he is going off to battle the dragon.

18. Who comes to Beowulf's assistance in his battle against the dragon?
    A. Wiglaf
    B. The slave who first awakened the anger of the dragon.
    C. No one comes to the assistance of Beowulf in his battle against the dragon.
    D. Hrothgar's two sons

19. What is Beowulf's dying wish?
    A. He wants peace in his country before he dies.
    B. He wishes to pardon all who have wronged him.
    C. He wants to see the dragon's treasure.
    D. He wishes to select Wiglaf as his successor.

20. What are Beowulf's instructions for after his funeral?
    A. He wants the Geats to build a large and lasting monument in his honor.
    B. He wishes to fade humbly into the past.
    C. He wishes to be entombed next to the dragon.
    D. He wants everyone to have a huge victory celebration in his honor.

Beowulf Multiple Choice Unit Test 2 Page 5

III. Composition

1. Who is the narrator of the *Beowulf* epic, and why is this important?

2. Describe the relationship between Beowulf and Unferth.

3. How does Beowulf's approach to fighting the dragon change from his attitude towards his battles with Grendel and his mother?

4. Could Beowulf have avoided his destiny, according to the beliefs of the Anglo-Saxons? Explain.

5. Discuss the significance of Grendel and his mother being called "the descendents of Cain."

6. How might the Christian monks have altered the original intent of the original *Beowulf* epic?

7. Discuss any significance to Beowulf's losing his power as he adorns more armor.

Beowulf Multiple Choice Unit Test 2 Page 6

IV. Vocabulary - Match the correct definitions to the words.

____ 1. tripartite	A.	prophetic signs
____ 2. ruminative	B.	a group or accumulation
____ 3. omens	C.	tight
____ 4. taut	D.	miserable, pitiable
____ 5. talons	E.	stones roughly placed together
____ 6. hilt	F.	the handle of a sword or dagger
____ 7. runic	G.	comfort in sorrow
____ 8. tarnish	H.	a repulsive old woman
____ 9. billowing	I.	a discoloration of metal
____ 10. malice	J.	evil intent
____ 11. hag	K.	made of dirt
____ 12. wretched	L.	bursting with flame or smoke
____ 13. earthen	M.	consisting of three parts
____ 14. unaided	N.	anxiety or concern
____ 15. belching	O.	meditative, pondering
____ 16. solace	P.	an ancient, interlacing script
____ 17. charring	Q.	burning
____ 18. hoards	R.	flowing, rising on the wind
____ 19. cobbled	S.	unassisted
____ 20. solicitude	T.	claws

ANSWER SHEET - *Beowulf*
Multiple Choice Unit Tests

I. Matching	II. Multiple Choice	IV. Vocabulary
1. ___	1. ___	1. ___
2. ___	2. ___	2. ___
3. ___	3. ___	3. ___
4. ___	4. ___	4. ___
5. ___	5. ___	5. ___
6. ___	6. ___	6. ___
7. ___	7. ___	7. ___
8. ___	8. ___	8. ___
9. ___	9. ___	9. ___
10. ___	10. ___	10. ___
11. ___	11. ___	11. ___
12. ___	12. ___	12. ___
13. ___	13. ___	13. ___
14. ___	14. ___	14. ___
15. ___	15. ___	15. ___
16. ___	16. ___	16. ___
17. ___	17. ___	17. ___
18. ___	18. ___	18. ___
19. ___	19. ___	19. ___
20. ___	20. ___	20. ___

ANSWER KEY - *Beowulf*
Multiple Choice Unit Test - 1

I. Matching	II. Multiple Choice	IV. Vocabulary
1. G	1. B	1. H
2. F	2. A	2. K
3. M	3. A	3. F
4. R	4. D	4. C
5. T	5. A	5. P
6. L	6. D	6. A
7. D	7. A	7. T
8. N	8. D	8. I
9. P	9. B	9. R
10. C	10. D	10. E
11. K	11. A	11. M
12. J	12. A	12. D
13. S	13. D	13. O
14. E	14. C	14. S
15. Q	15. B	15. L
16. I	16. A	16. Q
17. A	17. D	17. G
18. H	18. C	18. B
19. O	19. B	19. J
20. B	20. C	20. N

ANSWER KEY – *Beowulf*
Multiple Choice Unit Test – 2

I. Matching	II. Multiple Choice	IV. Vocabulary
1. G	1. B	1. M
2. D	2. D	2. O
3. J	3. C	3. A
4. H	4. B	4. C
5. A	5. D	5. T
6. L	6. A	6. F
7. F	7. C	7. P
8. P	8. B	8. I
9. N	9. B	9. R
10. B	10. A	10. J
11. S	11. B	11. H
12. M	12. C	12. D
13. K	13. A	13. K
14. E	14. C	14. S
15. Q	15. B	15. L
16. O	16. C	16. G
17. T	17. A	17. Q
18. R	18. A	18. C
19. I	19. C	19. E
20. C	20. A	20. N

UNIT RESOURCE MATERIALS

BULLETIN BOARD IDEAS - *Beowulf*

1. Save one corner of the board for the best of students' *Beowulf* writing assignments.

2. Take one of the word search puzzles from the extra activities packet and with a marker copy it over in a large size on the bulletin board. Write the clue words to find to one side. Invite students prior to and after class to find the words and circle them on the bulletin board.

3. Write several of the most significant quotations from the book onto the board on brightly colored paper.

4. Make a bulletin board listing the vocabulary words for this unit. As you complete sections of the novel and discuss the vocabulary for each section, write the definitions on the bulletin board. (If your board is one students face frequently, it will help them learn the words.)

5. Title the board: EPIC FEATURES. List and illustrate the epic features and their manifestation in *Beowulf* on the board.

6. Heraldry Board: Have students research and compose, and decorate a "coat of arms" for each of the major characters in *Beowulf* and post these on the board.

7. Title the board: FACES OF BEOWULF. Ask students to draw pictures of Beowulf, Grendel, Grendel's mother, and the dragon, based on the descriptions in the epic.

8. Create a map that corresponds to the events in the epic, Beowulf. Ask students to "age" the map and include the locations of all of the major points of action in the epic.

9. THEN AND NOW: Have students construct a bulletin board of the pagan influences in Beowulf (THEN) and how the poem was Christianized (NOW). Have then write passages from the poem to illustrate both then and now.

10. Create a kenning bulletin board. Ask students to write a definition of kennings on a large paper and put it in the center of the bulletin board. As students read *Beowulf*, they can write down kennings they find in the text and post them on the board as an on-going interactive assignment.

EXTRA ACTIVITIES - *Beowulf*

One of the difficulties in teaching a novel is that all students don't read at the same speed. One student who likes to read may take the book home and finish it in a day or two. Sometimes a few students finish the in-class assignments early. The problem, then, is finding suitable extra activities for students.

One thing that seems to help is to keep a little library in the classroom. For this unit on *Beowulf*, you might check out from the school library *Grendel,* by John Gardner, which is a modern version of the Beowulf story, told through the eyes of the monster, Grendel.

Other things you may keep on hand are puzzles. We have made some relating directly to *Beowulf* for you. Feel free to duplicate them for your students to use.

Some students may like to draw. You might devise a contest or allow some extra-credit grade for students who draw characters or scenes from *Beowulf*. Note, too, that if the students do not want to keep their drawings you may pick up some extra bulletin board materials this way. If you have a contest and you supply the prize (a CD or something like that perhaps), you could, possibly, make the drawing itself a non-returnable entry fee.

The pages which follow contain games, puzzles and worksheets. The keys, when appropriate, immediately follow the puzzle or worksheet. There are two main groups of activities: one group for the unit; that is, generally relating to *Beowulf* text, and another group of activities related strictly to *Beowulf* vocabulary.

Directions for these games, puzzles and worksheets are self-explanatory. The object here is to provide you with extra materials you may use in any way you choose.

MORE ACTIVITIES - *Beowulf*

1. Have students work together to make a time line chronology of the events in the story. Take a large piece of construction paper and on one wall (or however you can physically arrange it in your room) and make the events of the story along it. Students may want to add drawings or cut-out pictures to represent the events (as well as a written statement).

2. Have students design a book cover (front and back and inside flaps) for *Beowulf.*

3. Have students design a bulletin board (ready to be put up; not just sketched) for *Beowulf.*

4. Have students group the books together to show the larger structure of the novel. Have them explain why they chose the divisions they made.

5. Have students choose one book of the book (with sufficient dialogue) to rewrite as a play. In conjunction with this assignment, have students write a composition explaining the difficulties they encountered in changing from one written form to another.

6. Have students write a film script for *Beowulf,* and then write a composition in which they explain their rationale for casting the epic with the Hollywood actors of their choice.

7. Have students memorize and videotape a scene of their choice from *Beowulf* and show it to the class.

8. Have students research and hold a "medieval feast" such as one they would have during Anglo-Saxon times.

9. Have students write the opening installment of *Wiglaf,* an epic poem, which extols the virtues of the man who helped Beowulf slay the dragon.

10. Ask students to create a diorama of a scene from *Beowulf.*

11. Have students create a board game: FACES, PLACES, AND TRACES: in which the objective is to successfully complete three challenges and win the treasure. There should be three colors of squares on the board: Yellow for FACES—in which students have to identify characters from the work, Blue for PLACES, in which students must identify locations from Beowulf, and Red for TRACES, in which students must recall miscellaneous details from the epic.

Beowulf Word List

No.	Word	Clue/Definition
1.	ALLEGORY	A story told on two levels
2.	ALLITERATION	Repetition of initial consonant sound
3.	ANONYMOUS	The Beowulf author
4.	ARISTOCRATIC	The Class of society that Beowulf is concerned with
5.	BOASTFUL	Adjective that describes Unferth
6.	CAIN	Person that Grendel and his mom were descended from
7.	CAVE	Place where Grendel and his mother dwelled
8.	CHRISTIAN	Influences that inserted God into this initially pagan text
9.	CLAW	Only part of Grendel left at Herot after the fight with Beowulf
10.	COWARDS	What Wiglaf calls Beowulf's soldiers
11.	CUP	Taken by slave from the dragon
12.	DENMARK	Hrothgar's homeland
13.	EDGETHO	Beowulf's father
14.	EPIC	Long, narrative poem
15.	ESHER	Hrothgar's best friend; killed by Grendel's mother
16.	FAME	The only thing that lasts, according to the Anglo-Saxons
17.	FEASTS	Large parties that celebrate battle victories
18.	FEUDAL	Times of the Anglo-Saxons
19.	FIRES	What almost destroyed the last manuscript of Beowulf
20.	GEATLAND	Beowulf's homeland
21.	GOD	Beowulf's inspiration
22.	HERO	Lead characer of an epic; the protagonist
23.	HEROT	Hrothgar's mead hall
24.	HIGD	Higlac's wife
25.	HIGLAC	King of the Geats at the beginning of the epic
26.	HILT	Handle of a sword or dagger
27.	HORSEMEN	They rode around Beowulf's grave
28.	HROTHGAR	King of the Geats
29.	HRUNTING	Name of Unferth's sword
30.	KENNING	Anglo-Saxon metaphor
31.	LAKE	Grendel and his mom live at the bottom of this
32.	MAIL	Protective chains worn by Beowulf
33.	MONKS	They first put Beowulf in written form
34.	OMENS	Signs which predict the future
35.	ORAL	Beowulf was first sung in this tradition
36.	PAGAN	Beowulf's heathen origins
37.	PRIDE	What Hrothgar cautions Beowulf against
38.	PYRE	Funeral fire
39.	RAFFEL	Translator of Beowulf
40.	RHYTHM	The beat or cadence of the lines in poetry
41.	SERPENTS	What Beowulf encountered and slew on the way to Grendel's mother
42.	SIEGMUND	Earlier hero who also killed a dragon
43.	SLAVE	Awakened the sleeping dragon
44.	SWIMMING	Beowulf defeats Brecca in this competition
45.	TREASURE	It was guarded by the dragon
46.	TRIPARTITE	3-part story, such as Beowulf
47.	UNFERTH	He challenged Beowulf's swimming prowess
48.	WARRIOR	Type of person most prized in Anglo-Saxon society
49.	WELTHOW	Hrothgar's queen
50.	WULFGAR	Swedish prince who introduced Beowulf to Hrothgar

Beowulf Word Search

```
C G E A T L A N D A H I G D T W H T E B
H H R N W H K S E R L N C Z R A E J D W
R H U O U O D B V I L P N T I R R F G Y
I R S N L R B O A S T F U L P R O S E L
S O A Y F S W E L T H O W V A I T T T Y
T T E M G E P B S O K Q C M R O L N H M
I H R O A M G G C C M D Y Q T R I E O C
A G T U R E W N J R J C P L I S H P Y P
N A K S C N T L R A T Z L I T L H R K B
G R N O I T A R E T I L L A E S H E R N
N R R R P K C C C I B S L M W T N S R E
G N I M M I W S U C F L I D R N Q W R O
G O D R H Y T H M P E J J E I Y L Y L L
R P B X N S R S K G R D F N G P P A B T
A C Y Q A U G D O G F N G M F M R H K S
F O M E N S E R I F U E F A E O U I F E
F M F T I K Y A C N V P A R U T F N D T
E K I F A N H W Z A L I M K D Z J N D E
L N N F C O T O C Q M C E P A G A N W K
G S X H P M T C R L M W C A L G I H R G
```

ALLEGORY	EPIC	HORSEMEN	RHYTHM
ALLITERATION	ESHER	HROTHGAR	SERPENTS
ANONYMOUS	FAME	HRUNTING	SIEGMUND
ARISTOCRATIC	FEASTS	KENNING	SLAVE
BOASTFUL	FEUDAL	LAKE	SWIMMING
CAIN	FIRES	MAIL	TREASURE
CAVE	GEATLAND	MONKS	TRIPARTITE
CHRISTIAN	GOD	OMENS	UNFERTH
CLAW	HERO	ORAL	WARRIOR
COWARDS	HEROT	PAGAN	WELTHOW
CUP	HIGD	PRIDE	WULFGAR
DENMARK	HIGLAC	PYRE	
EDGETHO	HILT	RAFFEL	

Beowulf Word Search Answer Key

ALLEGORY	EPIC	HORSEMEN	RHYTHM
ALLITERATION	ESHER	HROTHGAR	SERPENTS
ANONYMOUS	FAME	HRUNTING	SIEGMUND
ARISTOCRATIC	FEASTS	KENNING	SLAVE
BOASTFUL	FEUDAL	LAKE	SWIMMING
CAIN	FIRES	MAIL	TREASURE
CAVE	GEATLAND	MONKS	TRIPARTITE
CHRISTIAN	GOD	OMENS	UNFERTH
CLAW	HERO	ORAL	WARRIOR
COWARDS	HEROT	PAGAN	WELTHOW
CUP	HIGD	PRIDE	WULFGAR
DENMARK	HIGLAC	PYRE	
EDGETHO	HILT	RAFFEL	

Beowulf Crossword

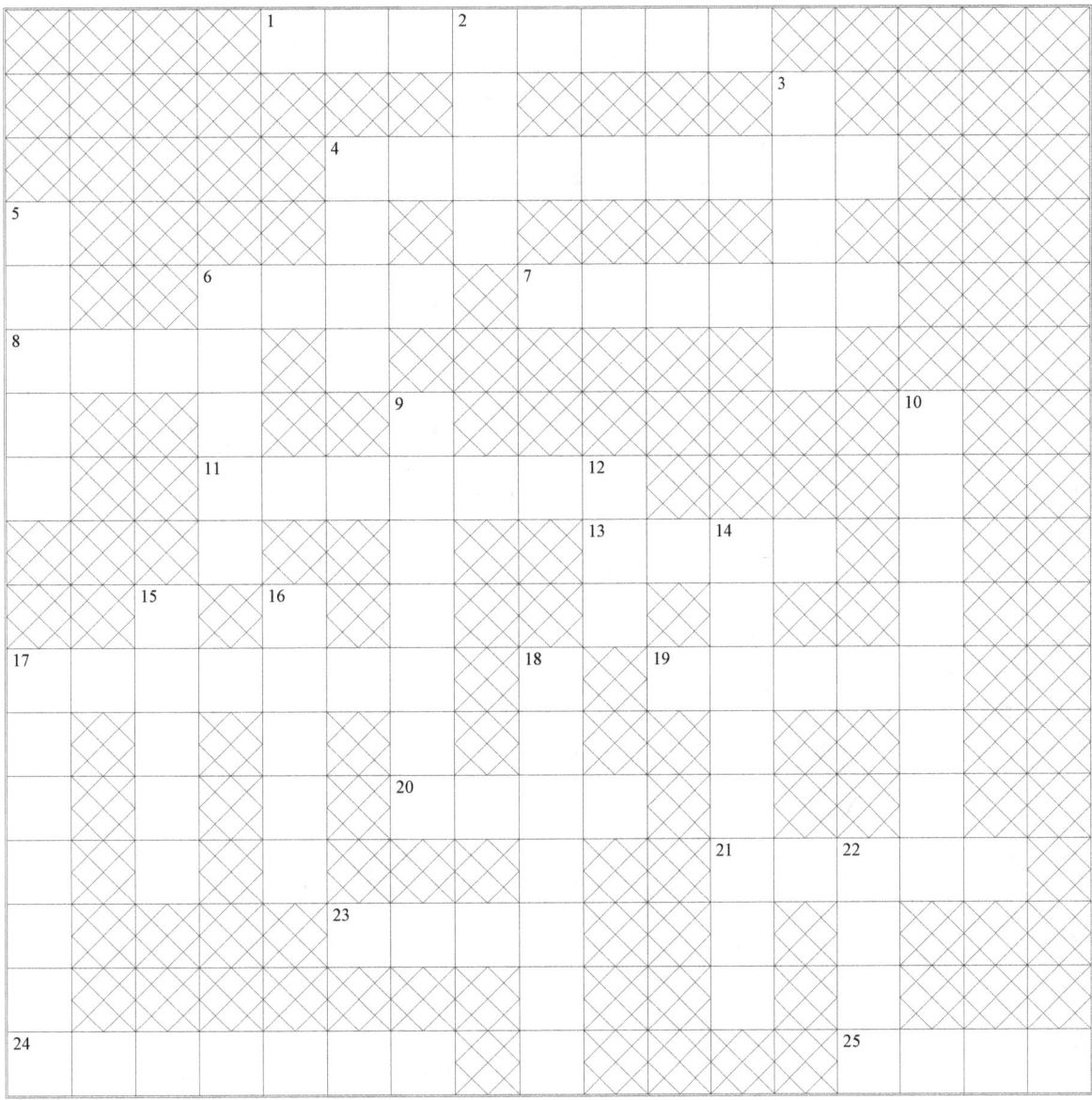

Across
1. What Beowulf encountered and slew on the way to Grendel's mother
4. Influences that inserted God into this initially pagan text
6. Protective chains worn by Beowulf
7. King of the Geats at the beginning of the epic
8. Lead characer of an epic; the protagonist
11. Anglo-Saxon metaphor
13. Beowulf was first sung in this tradition
17. Type of person most prized in Anglo-Saxon society
19. Awakened the sleeping dragon
20. Higlac's wife
21. Signs which predict the future
23. Handle of a sword or dagger
24. Swedish prince who introduced Beowulf to Hrothgar
25. Place where Grendel and his mother dwelled

Down
2. Funeral fire
3. Beowulf's heathen origins
4. Person that Grendel and his mom were descended from
5. Hrothgar's best friend; killed by Grendel's mother
6. They first put Beowulf in written form
9. He challenged Beowulf's swimming prowess
10. They rode around Beowulf's grave
12. Beowulf's inspiration
14. A story told on two levels
15. What Hrothgar cautions Beowulf against
16. What almost destroyed the last manuscript of Beowulf
17. Hrothgar's queen
18. Beowulf's father
22. Long, narrative poem

Beowulf Crossword Answer Key

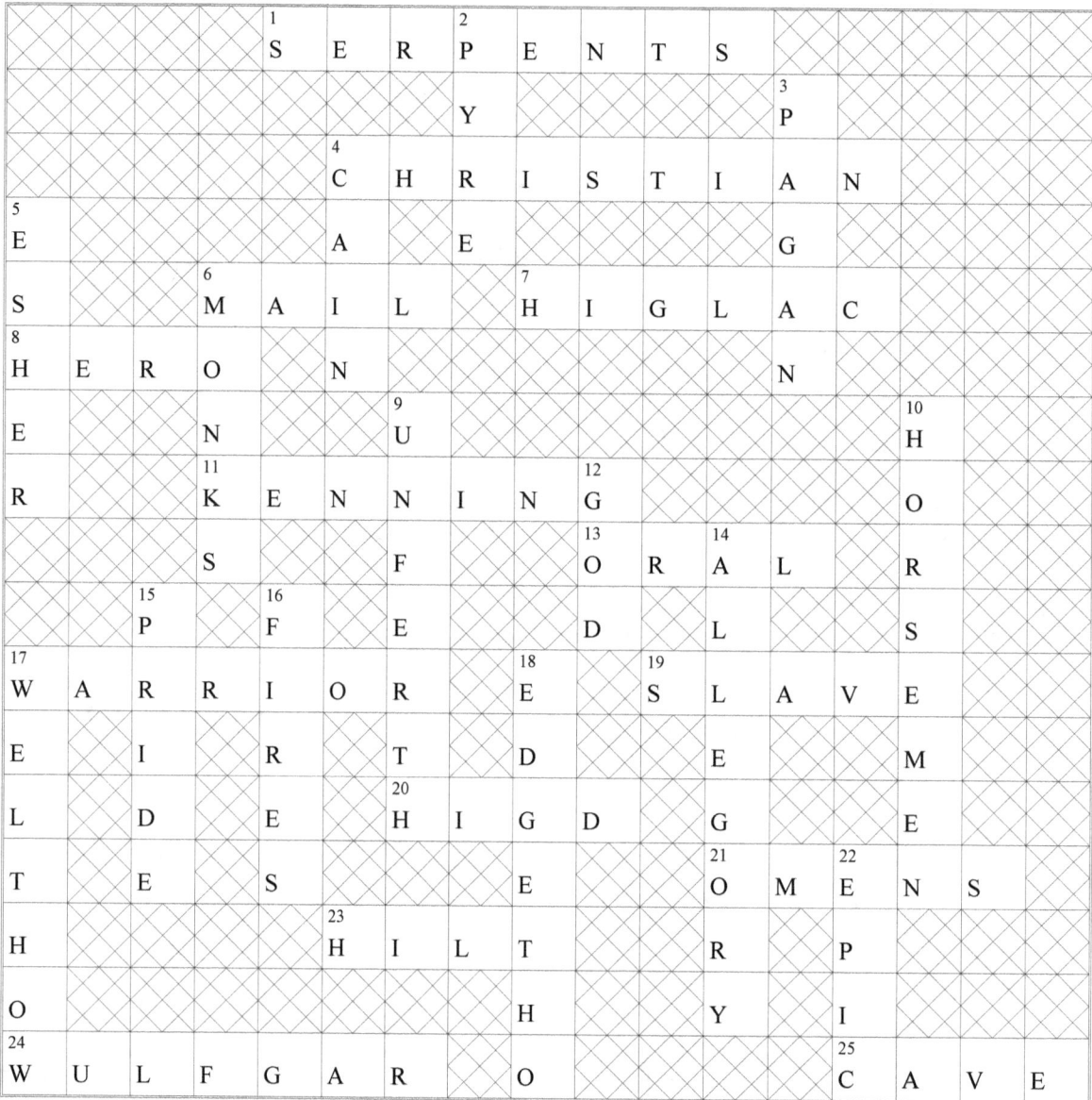

Across
1. What Beowulf encountered and slew on the way to Grendel's mother
4. Influences that inserted God into this initially pagan text
6. Protective chains worn by Beowulf
7. King of the Geats at the beginning of the epic
8. Lead characer of an epic; the protagonist
11. Anglo-Saxon metaphor
13. Beowulf was first sung in this tradition
17. Type of person most prized in Anglo-Saxon society
19. Awakened the sleeping dragon
20. Higlac's wife
21. Signs which predict the future
23. Handle of a sword or dagger
24. Swedish prince who introduced Beowulf to Hrothgar
25. Place where Grendel and his mother dwelled

Down
2. Funeral fire
3. Beowulf's heathen origins
4. Person that Grendel and his mom were descended from
5. Hrothgar's best friend; killed by Grendel's mother
6. They first put Beowulf in written form
9. He challenged Beowulf's swimming prowess
10. They rode around Beowulf's grave
12. Beowulf's inspiration
14. A story told on two levels
15. What Hrothgar cautions Beowulf against
16. What almost destroyed the last manuscript of Beowulf
17. Hrothgar's queen
18. Beowulf's father
22. Long, narrative poem

Beowulf Matching 1

___ 1. PAGAN   A. Earlier hero who also killed a dragon
___ 2. TRIPARTITE   B. Beowulf's father
___ 3. HILT   C. King of the Geats at the beginning of the epic
___ 4. WARRIOR   D. Hrothgar's homeland
___ 5. FIRES   E. Long, narrative poem
___ 6. ALLITERATION   F. Person that Grendel and his mom were descended from
___ 7. DENMARK   G. What Wiglaf calls Beowulf's soldiers
___ 8. GOD   H. What almost destroyed the last manuscript of Beowulf
___ 9. HIGLAC   I. 3-part story, such as Beowulf
___10. WULFGAR   J. Taken by slave from the dragon
___11. TREASURE   K. Awakened the sleeping dragon
___12. SLAVE   L. Beowulf's homeland
___13. SIEGMUND   M. Only part of Grendel left at Herot after the fight with Beowulf
___14. FEUDAL   N. Beowulf's heathen origins
___15. CAIN   O. Signs which predict the future
___16. CLAW   P. Repetition of initial consonant sound
___17. OMENS   Q. Hrothgar's queen
___18. COWARDS   R. Handle of a sword or dagger
___19. WELTHOW   S. Beowulf's inspiration
___20. CUP   T. Type of person most prized in Anglo-Saxon society
___21. GEATLAND   U. Swedish prince who introduced Beowulf to Hrothgar
___22. EDGETHO   V. Hrothgar's best friend; killed by Grendel's mother
___23. HEROT   W. It was guarded by the dragon
___24. EPIC   X. Times of the Anglo-Saxons
___25. ESHER   Y. Hrothgar's mead hall

Beowulf Matching 1 Answer Key

N - 1. PAGAN	A. Earlier hero who also killed a dragon
I - 2. TRIPARTITE	B. Beowulf's father
R - 3. HILT	C. King of the Geats at the beginning of the epic
T - 4. WARRIOR	D. Hrothgar's homeland
H - 5. FIRES	E. Long, narrative poem
P - 6. ALLITERATION	F. Person that Grendel and his mom were descended from
D - 7. DENMARK	G. What Wiglaf calls Beowulf's soldiers
S - 8. GOD	H. What almost destroyed the last manuscript of Beowulf
C - 9. HIGLAC	I. 3-part story, such as Beowulf
U -10. WULFGAR	J. Taken by slave from the dragon
W 11. TREASURE	K. Awakened the sleeping dragon
K -12. SLAVE	L. Beowulf's homeland
A -13. SIEGMUND	M. Only part of Grendel left at Herot after the fight with Beowulf
X -14. FEUDAL	N. Beowulf's heathen origins
F -15. CAIN	O. Signs which predict the future
M -16. CLAW	P. Repetition of initial consonant sound
O -17. OMENS	Q. Hrothgar's queen
G -18. COWARDS	R. Handle of a sword or dagger
Q -19. WELTHOW	S. Beowulf's inspiration
J - 20. CUP	T. Type of person most prized in Anglo-Saxon society
L -21. GEATLAND	U. Swedish prince who introduced Beowulf to Hrothgar
B -22. EDGETHO	V. Hrothgar's best friend; killed by Grendel's mother
Y -23. HEROT	W. It was guarded by the dragon
E -24. EPIC	X. Times of the Anglo-Saxons
V -25. ESHER	Y. Hrothgar's mead hall

Beowulf Matching 2

___ 1. EDGETHO   A. Beowulf defeats Brecca in this competition
___ 2. SWIMMING   B. Beowulf's homeland
___ 3. COWARDS   C. The only thing that lasts, according to the Anglo-Saxons
___ 4. KENNING   D. They rode around Beowulf's grave
___ 5. MAIL   E. It was guarded by the dragon
___ 6. LAKE   F. Awakened the sleeping dragon
___ 7. EPIC   G. Lead characer of an epic; the protagonist
___ 8. TREASURE   H. Protective chains worn by Beowulf
___ 9. CLAW   I. Higlac's wife
___10. ARISTOCRATIC   J. Handle of a sword or dagger
___11. CAVE   K. What Beowulf encountered and slew on the way to Grendel's mother
___12. SERPENTS   L. What Hrothgar cautions Beowulf against
___13. PRIDE   M. Earlier hero who also killed a dragon
___14. HILT   N. Only part of Grendel left at Herot after the fight with Beowulf
___15. HERO   O. Beowulf was first sung in this tradition
___16. FAME   P. Hrothgar's best friend; killed by Grendel's mother
___17. ESHER   Q. The beat or cadence of the lines in poetry
___18. HEROT   R. Anglo-Saxon metaphor
___19. SLAVE   S. Beowulf's father
___20. ORAL   T. The Class of society that Beowulf is concerned with
___21. SIEGMUND   U. What Wiglaf calls Beowulf's soldiers
___22. HORSEMEN   V. Place where Grendel and his mother dwelled
___23. GEATLAND   W. Grendel and his mom live at the bottom of this
___24. RHYTHM   X. Hrothgar's mead hall
___25. HIGD   Y. Long, narrative poem

Beowulf Matching 2 Answer Key

S - 1. EDGETHO		A. Beowulf defeats Brecca in this competition
A - 2. SWIMMING		B. Beowulf's homeland
U - 3. COWARDS		C. The only thing that lasts, according to the Anglo-Saxons
R - 4. KENNING		D. They rode around Beowulf's grave
H - 5. MAIL		E. It was guarded by the dragon
W - 6. LAKE		F. Awakened the sleeping dragon
Y - 7. EPIC		G. Lead characer of an epic; the protagonist
E - 8. TREASURE		H. Protective chains worn by Beowulf
N - 9. CLAW		I. Higlac's wife
T -10. ARISTOCRATIC		J. Handle of a sword or dagger
V -11. CAVE		K. What Beowulf encountered and slew on the way to Grendel's mother
K -12. SERPENTS		L. What Hrothgar cautions Beowulf against
L -13. PRIDE		M. Earlier hero who also killed a dragon
J - 14. HILT		N. Only part of Grendel left at Herot after the fight with Beowulf
G -15. HERO		O. Beowulf was first sung in this tradition
C -16. FAME		P. Hrothgar's best friend; killed by Grendel's mother
P -17. ESHER		Q. The beat or cadence of the lines in poetry
X -18. HEROT		R. Anglo-Saxon metaphor
F -19. SLAVE		S. Beowulf's father
O -20. ORAL		T. The Class of society that Beowulf is concerned with
M 21. SIEGMUND		U. What Wiglaf calls Beowulf's soldiers
D -22. HORSEMEN		V. Place where Grendel and his mother dwelled
B -23. GEATLAND		W. Grendel and his mom live at the bottom of this
Q -24. RHYTHM		X. Hrothgar's mead hall
I - 25. HIGD		Y. Long, narrative poem

Beowulf Juggle Letters 1

1. EKLA = 1. _____
   Grendel and his mom live at the bottom of this

2. ROHE = 2. _____
   Lead characer of an epic; the protagonist

3. NUTHREF = 3. _____
   He challenged Beowulf's swimming prowess

4. NICA = 4. _____
   Person that Grendel and his mom were descended from

5. SNOREEHM = 5. _____
   They rode around Beowulf's grave

6. EHSER = 6. _____
   Hrothgar's best friend; killed by Grendel's mother

7. NHNURIGT = 7. _____
   Name of Unferth's sword

8. OGD = 8. _____
   Beowulf's inspiration

9. EISRF = 9. _____
   What almost destroyed the last manuscript of Beowulf

10. FRFALE =10. _____
    Translator of Beowulf

11. IRRTATCACSIO =11. _____
    The Class of society that Beowulf is concerned with

12. TSSAEF =12. _____
    Large parties that celebrate battle victories

13. DLAUFE =13. _____
    Times of the Anglo-Saxons

14. CILHAG =14. _____
    King of the Geats at the beginning of the epic

15. GOHTEED =15. _____
    Beowulf's father

16. AGPNA =16. _____
Beowulf's heathen origins

17. RLEIAONTLITA =17. _____
Repetition of initial consonant sound

18. TSERPESN =18. _____
What Beowulf encountered and slew on the way to Grendel's mother

19. IECP =19. _____
Long, narrative poem

20. NNAMSYOOU =20. _____
The Beowulf author

21. LVAES =21. _____
Awakened the sleeping dragon

22. AMKDNRE =22. _____
Hrothgar's homeland

23. HOLWWTE =23. _____
Hrothgar's queen

24. EMFA =24. _____
The only thing that lasts, according to the Anglo-Saxons

25. EDPIR =25. _____
What Hrothgar cautions Beowulf against

Beowulf Juggle Letters 1 Answer Key

1. EKLA = 1. LAKE
   Grendel and his mom live at the bottom of this

2. ROHE = 2. HERO
   Lead characer of an epic; the protagonist

3. NUTHREF = 3. UNFERTH
   He challenged Beowulf's swimming prowess

4. NICA = 4. CAIN
   Person that Grendel and his mom were descended from

5. SNOREEHM = 5. HORSEMEN
   They rode around Beowulf's grave

6. EHSER = 6. ESHER
   Hrothgar's best friend; killed by Grendel's mother

7. NHNURIGT = 7. HRUNTING
   Name of Unferth's sword

8. OGD = 8. GOD
   Beowulf's inspiration

9. EISRF = 9. FIRES
   What almost destroyed the last manuscript of Beowulf

10. FRFALE =10. RAFFEL
    Translator of Beowulf

11. IRRTATCACSIO =11. ARISTOCRATIC
    The Class of society that Beowulf is concerned with

12. TSSAEF =12. FEASTS
    Large parties that celebrate battle victories

13. DLAUFE =13. FEUDAL
    Times of the Anglo-Saxons

14. CILHAG =14. HIGLAC
    King of the Geats at the beginning of the epic

15. GOHTEED =15. EDGETHO
    Beowulf's father

16. AGPNA =16. PAGAN
Beowulf's heathen origins

17. RLEIAONTLITA =17. ALLITERATION
Repetition of initial consonant sound

18. TSERPESN =18. SERPENTS
What Beowulf encountered and slew on the way to Grendel's mother

19. IECP =19. EPIC
Long, narrative poem

20. NNAMSYOOU =20. ANONYMOUS
The Beowulf author

21. LVAES =21. SLAVE
Awakened the sleeping dragon

22. AMKDNRE =22. DENMARK
Hrothgar's homeland

23. HOLWWTE =23. WELTHOW
Hrothgar's queen

24. EMFA =24. FAME
The only thing that lasts, according to the Anglo-Saxons

25. EDPIR =25. PRIDE
What Hrothgar cautions Beowulf against

Beowulf Juggle Letters 2

1. AILM = 1. _____
Protective chains worn by Beowulf

2. INKGENN = 2. _____
Anglo-Saxon metaphor

3. WCLA = 3. _____
Only part of Grendel left at Herot after the fight with Beowulf

4. RYEP = 4. _____
Funeral fire

5. NIMMISGW = 5. _____
Beowulf defeats Brecca in this competition

6. AYLERLGO = 6. _____
A story told on two levels

7. TARRPEITTI = 7. _____
3-part story, such as Beowulf

8. PCU = 8. _____
Taken by slave from the dragon

9. HNCIAIRTS = 9. _____
Influences that inserted God into this initially pagan text

10. KNOMS =10. _____
They first put Beowulf in written form

11. ACODWRS =11. _____
What Wiglaf calls Beowulf's soldiers

12. RRGHHTOA =12. _____
King of the Geats

13. RAIORWR =13. _____
Type of person most prized in Anglo-Saxon society

14. AECV =14. _____
Place where Grendel and his mother dwelled

15. THHRYM =15. _____
The beat or cadence of the lines in poetry

16. GWULRAF =16. _____
Swedish prince who introduced Beowulf to Hrothgar

17. TORHE =17. _____
Hrothgar's mead hall

18. IGHD =18. _____
Higlac's wife

19. AFOBLTSU =19. _____
Adjective that describes Unferth

20. DNELAAGT =20. _____
Beowulf's homeland

21. UATERRSE =21. _____
It was guarded by the dragon

22. EIDMUGSN =22. _____
Earlier hero who also killed a dragon

23. RALO =23. _____
Beowulf was first sung in this tradition

24. SOMNE =24. _____
Signs which predict the future

25. THIL =25. _____
Handle of a sword or dagger

Beowulf Juggle Letters 2 Answer Key

1. AILM = 1. MAIL
   Protective chains worn by Beowulf

2. INKGENN = 2. KENNING
   Anglo-Saxon metaphor

3. WCLA = 3. CLAW
   Only part of Grendel left at Herot after the fight with Beowulf

4. RYEP = 4. PYRE
   Funeral fire

5. NIMMISGW = 5. SWIMMING
   Beowulf defeats Brecca in this competition

6. AYLERLGO = 6. ALLEGORY
   A story told on two levels

7. TARRPEITTI = 7. TRIPARTITE
   3-part story, such as Beowulf

8. PCU = 8. CUP
   Taken by slave from the dragon

9. HNCIAIRTS = 9. CHRISTIAN
   Influences that inserted God into this initially pagan text

10. KNOMS =10. MONKS
    They first put Beowulf in written form

11. ACODWRS =11. COWARDS
    What Wiglaf calls Beowulf's soldiers

12. RRGHHTOA =12. HROTHGAR
    King of the Geats

13. RAIORWR =13. WARRIOR
    Type of person most prized in Anglo-Saxon society

14. AECV =14. CAVE
    Place where Grendel and his mother dwelled

15. THHRYM =15. RHYTHM
    The beat or cadence of the lines in poetry

16. GWULRAF	=16.	WULFGAR
		Swedish prince who introduced Beowulf to Hrothgar
17. TORHE	=17.	HEROT
		Hrothgar's mead hall
18. IGHD	=18.	HIGD
		Higlac's wife
19. AFOBLTSU	=19.	BOASTFUL
		Adjective that describes Unferth
20. DNELAAGT	=20.	GEATLAND
		Beowulf's homeland
21. UATERRSE	=21.	TREASURE
		It was guarded by the dragon
22. EIDMUGSN	=22.	SIEGMUND
		Earlier hero who also killed a dragon
23. RALO	=23.	ORAL
		Beowulf was first sung in this tradition
24. SOMNE	=24.	OMENS
		Signs which predict the future
25. THIL	=25.	HILT
		Handle of a sword or dagger

VOCABULARY RESOURCE MATERIALS

Beowulf Vocabulary Word List

No.	Word	Clue/Definition
1.	ASCRIBED	Attributed; assigned
2.	BELCHING	Bursting with flame or smoke
3.	BILLOWING	Flowing, rising on the winds
4.	CHARRING	Burning
5.	COBBLED	Stones roughly placed together
6.	COMPELLED	Forced
7.	DECREED	Ordered by a judge
8.	DISSOLUTION	Dispersal
9.	EARTHEN	Made of dirt
10.	ELUCIDATE	Make clear
11.	EMULATED	Rival with some degree of success
12.	EXULTING	Rejoicing triumphantly
13.	FURROWS	Narrow, trench-like depressions
14.	GROPED	Searched for blindly
15.	HAG	Repulsive old woman
16.	HALTINGLY	With hesitation
17.	HEATHEN	Pagan; non-Christian
18.	HILT	Handle of a sword or dagger
19.	HOARDS	A group or accumulation
20.	JACKAL	One who meanly serves the purpose of another
21.	LINDEN	Trees with heart-shaped leaves
22.	MALICE	Evil intent
23.	NIGGARDLY	Stingy
24.	OMENS	Signs of things to come
25.	PYRE	Pile of wood for burning dead bodies
26.	REPARATION	Process of making amends
27.	REPRISAL	Retaliation; revenge
28.	RUMINATIVE	Meditative; pondering
29.	RUNIC	Ancient, interlacing script
30.	SCABBARD	Sheath or cover for a sword
31.	SOLACE	Comfort in sorrow
32.	SOLICITUDE	Anxiety or concern
33.	TALONS	Claws
34.	TARNISH	Discoloration of metal
35.	TAUT	Tight
36.	TRIPARTITE	Consisting of three parts
37.	UNAIDED	Without help
38.	VENOM	Poison
39.	WRETCHED	Miserable; pitiable
40.	WRITHING	Twisting and squirming

Beowulf Vocabulary Word Search

Words are placed backwards, forward, diagonally, up and down. Words listed below are included in the maze. Circle the hidden vocabulary words in the maze.

```
G F U R R O W S T T J H B M G V P V E X
R R E P A R A T I O N N A L N G G Z A R
O M V K Y C G K U W K B W L I R M Y R V
P B I L L O W I N G P Y R E T N X J T B
E N T C V M C R A A D R I E L I Z P H C
D K A H R P T E I S Z Z T M U G N S E V
E D N A B E F P D C Q G H U X G S G N C
C T I R C L B R E R K K I L E A C H L F
R R M R H L H I D I E G N A E R A D F Y
E I U I T E X S B B D H G T X D B T X J
E P R N L D B A D E U D A E S L B V T W
D A X G W Y N L Q D T D J D R Y A G V P
H R W R Q E D X N T I L N A M V R N L M
G T V X H B Y H Y C C B K P C C D I N T
Y I R T X H S R U L I C S Y D K N H H S
Q T A U S I I L F Q L N T V Q D A C O Z
L E W R N D E L B B O C A F E C I L A M
H S H R E I N B T L S W U N J N A E R Z
H K A N M L C N A N P V T K P C O B D W
H T G L O D B T W R E T C H E D F M S Z
```

ASCRIBED	EXULTING	MALICE	SOLICITUDE
BELCHING	FURROWS	NIGGARDLY	TALONS
BILLOWING	GROPED	OMENS	TARNISH
CHARRING	HAG	PYRE	TAUT
COBBLED	HALTINGLY	REPARATION	TRIPARTITE
COMPELLED	HEATHEN	REPRISAL	UNAIDED
DECREED	HILT	RUMINATIVE	VENOM
EARTHEN	HOARDS	RUNIC	WRETCHED
ELUCIDATE	JACKAL	SCABBARD	WRITHING
EMULATED	LINDEN	SOLACE	

Beowulf Vocabulary Word Search Answer Key

Words are placed backwards, forward, diagonally, up and down. Words listed below are included in the maze. Circle the hidden vocabulary words in the maze.

ASCRIBED	EXULTING	MALICE	SOLICITUDE
BELCHING	FURROWS	NIGGARDLY	TALONS
BILLOWING	GROPED	OMENS	TARNISH
CHARRING	HAG	PYRE	TAUT
COBBLED	HALTINGLY	REPARATION	TRIPARTITE
COMPELLED	HEATHEN	REPRISAL	UNAIDED
DECREED	HILT	RUMINATIVE	VENOM
EARTHEN	HOARDS	RUNIC	WRETCHED
ELUCIDATE	JACKAL	SCABBARD	WRITHING
EMULATED	LINDEN	SOLACE	

Beowulf Vocabulary Crossword

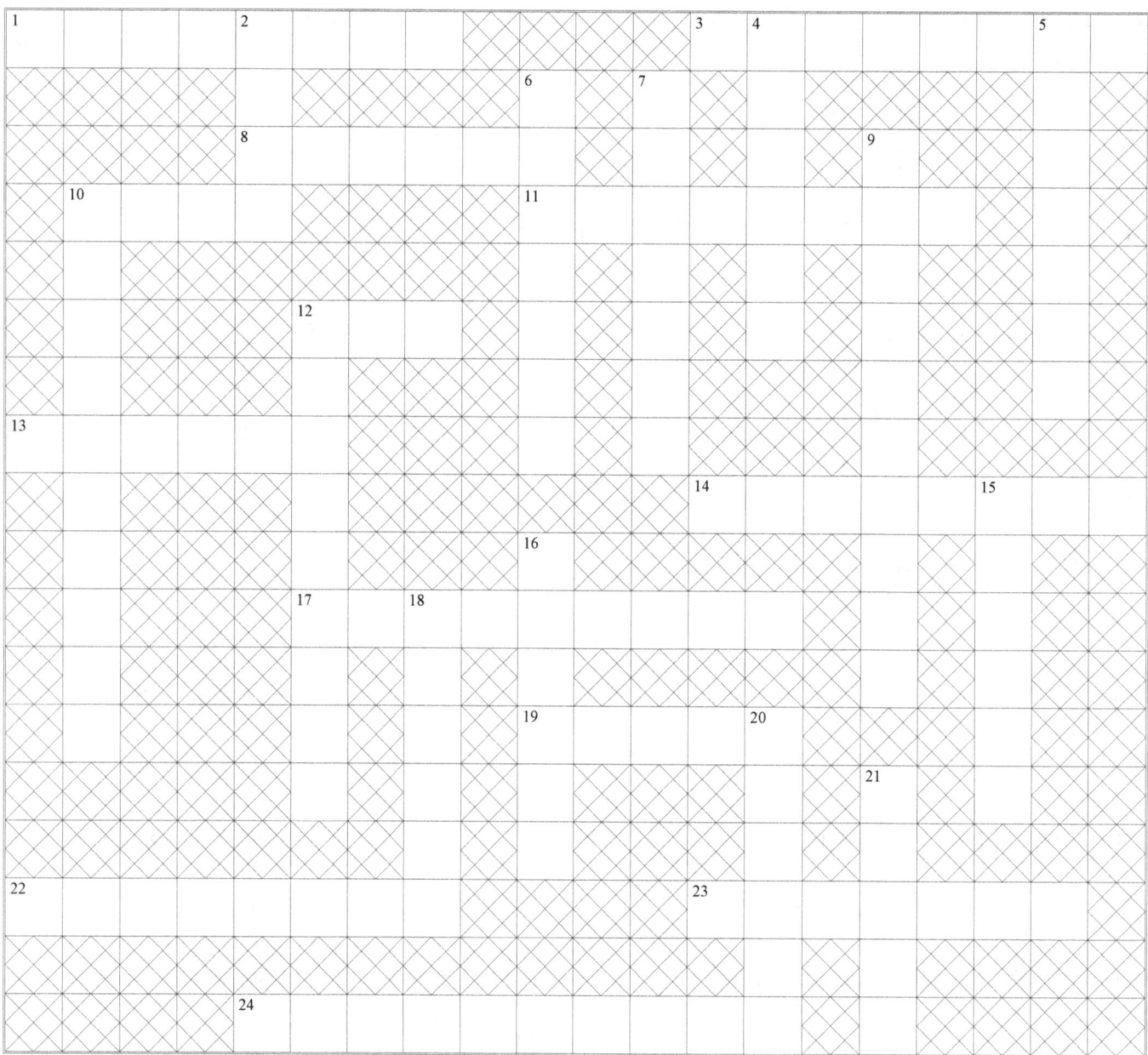

Across
1. Twisting and squirming
3. Rival with some degree of success
8. Trees with heart-shaped leaves
10. Tight
11. Attributed; assigned
12. Repulsive old woman
13. One who meanly serves the purpose of another
14. Miserable; pitiable
17. Stingy
19. Signs of things to come
22. Sheath or cover for a sword
23. Discoloration of metal
24. Anxiety or concern

Down
2. Handle of a sword or dagger
4. Evil intent
5. Made of dirt
6. Without help
7. Ordered by a judge
9. Process of making amends
10. Consisting of three parts
12. With hesitation
15. A group or accumulation
16. Claws
18. Searched for blindly
20. Comfort in sorrow
21. Ancient, interlacing script

Beowulf Vocabulary Crossword Answer Key

	1 W	R	I	2 T H	I	N	G			3 E	4 M	U	L	A	T	5 E	D
				I				6 U		7 D		A				A	
				8 L	I	N	D	E	N	E		L		9 R		R	
	10 T	A	U	T				11 A	S	C	R	I	B	E	D	T	
	R							I		R		C		P		H	
	I			12 H	A	G		D		E		E		A		E	
	P			A				E		E				R		N	
13 J	A	C	K	A	L			D		D				A			
	R			T						14 W	R	E	T	15 C	H	E	D
	T			I			16 T							I		O	
	I			17 N	I	18 G	G	A	R	D	L	Y		O		A	
	T			G		R		L						N		R	
	E			L		O		19 O	M	E	N	20 S				D	
				Y		P		N				O		21 R		S	
						E		S				L		U			
22 S	C	A	B	B	A	R	D			23 T	A	R	N	I	S	H	
										C				I			
			24 S	O	L	I	C	I	T	U	D	E		C			

Across
1. Twisting and squirming
3. Rival with some degree of success
8. Trees with heart-shaped leaves
10. Tight
11. Attributed; assigned
12. Repulsive old woman
13. One who meanly serves the purpose of another
14. Miserable; pitiable
17. Stingy
19. Signs of things to come
22. Sheath or cover for a sword
23. Discoloration of metal
24. Anxiety or concern

Down
2. Handle of a sword or dagger
4. Evil intent
5. Made of dirt
6. Without help
7. Ordered by a judge
9. Process of making amends
10. Consisting of three parts
12. With hesitation
15. A group or accumulation
16. Claws
18. Searched for blindly
20. Comfort in sorrow
21. Ancient, interlacing script

Beowulf Vocabulary Matching 1

___ 1. COMPELLED   A. Rejoicing triumphantly
___ 2. DISSOLUTION   B. Sheath or cover for a sword
___ 3. TAUT   C. Comfort in sorrow
___ 4. SCABBARD   D. Dispersal
___ 5. HILT   E. Forced
___ 6. UNAIDED   F. Process of making amends
___ 7. GROPED   G. One who meanly serves the purpose of another
___ 8. REPARATION   H. Stones roughly placed together
___ 9. PYRE   I. Miserable; pitiable
___10. JACKAL   J. Without help
___11. HALTINGLY   K. Bursting with flame or smoke
___12. BELCHING   L. With hesitation
___13. DECREED   M. Tight
___14. COBBLED   N. Meditative; pondering
___15. RUMINATIVE   O. Claws
___16. SOLICITUDE   P. Handle of a sword or dagger
___17. REPRISAL   Q. Ordered by a judge
___18. EXULTING   R. Make clear
___19. SOLACE   S. Pile of wood for burning dead bodies
___20. WRETCHED   T. Searched for blindly
___21. TALONS   U. Made of dirt
___22. ELUCIDATE   V. Retaliation; revenge
___23. CHARRING   W. Burning
___24. EARTHEN   X. Anxiety or concern
___25. LINDEN   Y. Trees with heart-shaped leaves

Beowulf Vocabulary Matching 1 Answer Key

E - 1.	COMPELLED	A. Rejoicing triumphantly
D - 2.	DISSOLUTION	B. Sheath or cover for a sword
M - 3.	TAUT	C. Comfort in sorrow
B - 4.	SCABBARD	D. Dispersal
P - 5.	HILT	E. Forced
J - 6.	UNAIDED	F. Process of making amends
T - 7.	GROPED	G. One who meanly serves the purpose of another
F - 8.	REPARATION	H. Stones roughly placed together
S - 9.	PYRE	I. Miserable; pitiable
G - 10.	JACKAL	J. Without help
L - 11.	HALTINGLY	K. Bursting with flame or smoke
K - 12.	BELCHING	L. With hesitation
Q - 13.	DECREED	M. Tight
H - 14.	COBBLED	N. Meditative; pondering
N - 15.	RUMINATIVE	O. Claws
X - 16.	SOLICITUDE	P. Handle of a sword or dagger
V - 17.	REPRISAL	Q. Ordered by a judge
A - 18.	EXULTING	R. Make clear
C - 19.	SOLACE	S. Pile of wood for burning dead bodies
I - 20.	WRETCHED	T. Searched for blindly
O - 21.	TALONS	U. Made of dirt
R - 22.	ELUCIDATE	V. Retaliation; revenge
W 23.	CHARRING	W. Burning
U - 24.	EARTHEN	X. Anxiety or concern
Y - 25.	LINDEN	Y. Trees with heart-shaped leaves

Beowulf Vocabulary Matching 2

___ 1. GROPED   A. Signs of things to come
___ 2. HOARDS   B. With hesitation
___ 3. RUMINATIVE   C. Burning
___ 4. SOLICITUDE   D. Searched for blindly
___ 5. CHARRING   E. A group or accumulation
___ 6. BILLOWING   F. Flowing, rising on the winds
___ 7. HILT   G. Process of making amends
___ 8. TRIPARTITE   H. Meditative; pondering
___ 9. SCABBARD   I. Rejoicing triumphantly
___ 10. DISSOLUTION   J. Claws
___ 11. HAG   K. Handle of a sword or dagger
___ 12. WRITHING   L. Repulsive old woman
___ 13. TALONS   M. Made of dirt
___ 14. MALICE   N. Stingy
___ 15. FURROWS   O. Ordered by a judge
___ 16. NIGGARDLY   P. Without help
___ 17. REPARATION   Q. Sheath or cover for a sword
___ 18. EXULTING   R. Consisting of three parts
___ 19. OMENS   S. Dispersal
___ 20. UNAIDED   T. Comfort in sorrow
___ 21. HALTINGLY   U. Narrow, trench-like depressions
___ 22. EARTHEN   V. Evil intent
___ 23. DECREED   W. Anxiety or concern
___ 24. JACKAL   X. Twisting and squirming
___ 25. SOLACE   Y. One who meanly serves the purpose of another

Beowulf Vocabulary Matching 2 Answer Key

D - 1.	GROPED	A. Signs of things to come
E - 2.	HOARDS	B. With hesitation
H - 3.	RUMINATIVE	C. Burning
W 4.	SOLICITUDE	D. Searched for blindly
C - 5.	CHARRING	E. A group or accumulation
F - 6.	BILLOWING	F. Flowing, rising on the winds
K - 7.	HILT	G. Process of making amends
R - 8.	TRIPARTITE	H. Meditative; pondering
Q - 9.	SCABBARD	I. Rejoicing triumphantly
S - 10.	DISSOLUTION	J. Claws
L - 11.	HAG	K. Handle of a sword or dagger
X - 12.	WRITHING	L. Repulsive old woman
J - 13.	TALONS	M. Made of dirt
V - 14.	MALICE	N. Stingy
U - 15.	FURROWS	O. Ordered by a judge
N - 16.	NIGGARDLY	P. Without help
G - 17.	REPARATION	Q. Sheath or cover for a sword
I - 18.	EXULTING	R. Consisting of three parts
A - 19.	OMENS	S. Dispersal
P - 20.	UNAIDED	T. Comfort in sorrow
B - 21.	HALTINGLY	U. Narrow, trench-like depressions
M 22.	EARTHEN	V. Evil intent
O - 23.	DECREED	W. Anxiety or concern
Y - 24.	JACKAL	X. Twisting and squirming
T - 25.	SOLACE	Y. One who meanly serves the purpose of another

Beowulf Vocabulary Juggle Letters 1

1. GAH = 1. _____
   Repulsive old woman

2. AEIUDDN = 2. _____
   Without help

3. ARIYDGLGN = 3. _____
   Stingy

4. ATTU = 4. _____
   Tight

5. CIERSADB = 5. _____
   Attributed; assigned

6. ISARNTH = 6. _____
   Discoloration of metal

7. VNMOE = 7. _____
   Poison

8. LHIT = 8. _____
   Handle of a sword or dagger

9. LAJKCA = 9. _____
   One who meanly serves the purpose of another

10. NTUEXIGL =10. _____
    Rejoicing triumphantly

11. RHEAETN =11. _____
    Made of dirt

12. TRGINHIW =12. _____
    Twisting and squirming

13. ECLAIM =13. _____
    Evil intent

14. NOALST =14. _____
    Claws

15. AASBBRDC =15. _____
    Sheath or cover for a sword

Beowulf Vocabulary Juggle Letters 1 Answer Key

1. GAH = 1. HAG
Repulsive old woman

2. AEIUDDN = 2. UNAIDED
Without help

3. ARIYDGLGN = 3. NIGGARDLY
Stingy

4. ATTU = 4. TAUT
Tight

5. CIERSADB = 5. ASCRIBED
Attributed; assigned

6. ISARNTH = 6. TARNISH
Discoloration of metal

7. VNMOE = 7. VENOM
Poison

8. LHIT = 8. HILT
Handle of a sword or dagger

9. LAJKCA = 9. JACKAL
One who meanly serves the purpose of another

10. NTUEXIGL = 10. EXULTING
Rejoicing triumphantly

11. RHEAETN = 11. EARTHEN
Made of dirt

12. TRGINHIW = 12. WRITHING
Twisting and squirming

13. ECLAIM = 13. MALICE
Evil intent

14. NOALST = 14. TALONS
Claws

15. AASBBRDC = 15. SCABBARD
Sheath or cover for a sword

Beowulf Vocabulary Juggle Letters 2

1. IARTVUINEM = 1. _____
   Meditative; pondering

2. ECOALS = 2. _____
   Comfort in sorrow

3. NEMOS = 3. _____
   Signs of things to come

4. NSHRIAT = 4. _____
   Discoloration of metal

5. ICDERBAS = 5. _____
   Attributed; assigned

6. OADRSH = 6. _____
   A group or accumulation

7. AHG = 7. _____
   Repulsive old woman

8. TWGIIHNR = 8. _____
   Twisting and squirming

9. ATIEUDELC = 9. _____
   Make clear

10. RNETEHA =10. _____
    Made of dirt

11. INUDEDA =11. _____
    Without help

12. DEECTWRH =12. _____
    Miserable; pitiable

13. ITUIOODSNLS =13. _____
    Dispersal

14. LGXITNUE =14. _____
    Rejoicing triumphantly

15. NTOSLA =15. _____
    Claws

Beowulf Vocabulary Juggle Letters 2 Answer Key

1. IARTVUINEM = 1. RUMINATIVE
   Meditative; pondering

2. ECOALS = 2. SOLACE
   Comfort in sorrow

3. NEMOS = 3. OMENS
   Signs of things to come

4. NSHRIAT = 4. TARNISH
   Discoloration of metal

5. ICDERBAS = 5. ASCRIBED
   Attributed; assigned

6. OADRSH = 6. HOARDS
   A group or accumulation

7. AHG = 7. HAG
   Repulsive old woman

8. TWGIIHNR = 8. WRITHING
   Twisting and squirming

9. ATIEUDELC = 9. ELUCIDATE
   Make clear

10. RNETEHA =10. EARTHEN
    Made of dirt

11. INUDEDA =11. UNAIDED
    Without help

12. DEECTWRH =12. WRETCHED
    Miserable; pitiable

13. ITUIOODSNLS =13. DISSOLUTION
    Dispersal

14. LGXITNUE =14. EXULTING
    Rejoicing triumphantly

15. NTOSLA =15. TALONS
    Claws

www.ingramcontent.com/pod-product-compliance
Lightning Source LLC
Chambersburg PA
CBHW051408070526
44584CB00023B/3344